Best Wishes
David Maclennan.

All the best!
Dave Anderson.

ROADWORKS

SONG LYRICS FOR WILDCAT
BY DAVID ANDERSON AND DAVID MACLENNAN

Selected by Edwin Morgan

Third Eye Centre
1987

ROADWORKS

Song Lyrics for Wildcat
by David Anderson and David MacLennan

Selected by Edwin Morgan

First published May 1987 in an
edition of 2000 paperback copies
ISBN 0 906474 66 3

Anderson, David
Roadworks: songs lyrics for Wildcat.
1 Music, Popular (songs, etc.) — Texts
I Title II. MacLennan, David III. Morgan, Edwin IV.
Wildcat Music Theatre Company 784.5'05 ML54.6
ISBN 0 906474 66 3

Roadworks is subsidised by the Scottish Arts Council
Roadworks is co-funded by the STUC

Edited by David Anderson, David MacLennan,
Annette Gillies and Christopher Carrell
Photographs selected by Christopher Carrell
Layout and design by Annette Gillies
Published by Third Eye Centre (Glasgow) Ltd.
in association with the STUC
Printed by E.F. Peterson, 12 Laygate,
South Shields, Tyne and Wear
Distributed by Third Eye Centre,
350 Sauchiehall Street, Glasgow G2 3JD
041 332 7521

PREFACE

There are many people to thank for this book of lyrics. Tina Anderson for putting up with hours of piano thumping late into the night. Feri Lean for helping us to start Wildcat. All the 'Musos' over the years who have played and sung the songs. Chris Carrell for suggesting we collect the lyrics in a book, Edwin Morgan for selecting them and Liz Lochhead for helping us prepare them for the page. Phyllis Steele for typing the words, Annette Gillies for design and layout, and Brenda Carson for acting as mid-wife to the publication. Oscar Marzaroli for photographs on the back and front covers and George Oliver, Tom Hilton, Sean Hudson, Dave Williams, Alan Wylie, Antonia Reeves, Anthony Brannan for their production stills. Thanks also to the STUC for financial support and to the Scottish Arts Council for their subsidy.

The biggest thank you is to the Wildcat audience who have enjoyed the songs and encouraged us to write more.

David Anderson
David MacLennan

CONTENTS

The Complete History of Rock 'N' Roll   Photo George Oliver
Opening Night Third Eye Centre

INTRODUCTION

The first time I ever heard of Wildcat was in a letter from home my sister sent me in the Autumn of 1978 just after I'd gone to Canada on a year-long Scottish Arts Council Writers' exchange scheme. " . . . Remember that guy? Well, he asked me out and he'd got tickets for Wildcat — that's some of the people from 7:84 who've broken away to have a new company based on rock music — that girl Terry is absolutely amazing, what a voice — and they've got a new show called *The Painted Bird* which is all about how we judge and treat the mentally ill and drugs and big profits for pharmaceutical companies and suppression and it was absolutely brilliant." Even allowing for first date euphoria and her obvious keenness to award "that guy" (she married him not all that long after) ten out of ten for not taking her "somewhere boring and ordinary like the pictures", I did gather that she, like most people (and the critics too), had been very, very impressed by this new departure.

I can't imagine, though, that *The Painted Bird* could have possibly caused such a sensation as 7:84 (Scotland) Theatre Company's *The Cheviot, The Stag, and The Black Black Oil* did only five years earlier. Simply because in that five years an audience had evolved which was well used to the epic and the episodic; to shifting styles of narration; to monologues and music interrupting the action; to having their heartstrings tugged one minute, their funnybones tickled the next; to being addressed directly over the footlights and not ignored behind an invisible 'fourth wall'; to being wide open to styles other than naturalism; to there being no reason why something could not be simultaneously thoroughly entertaining and serious-and-thought-provoking. Of course 7:84 would never — could never — claim to have created these 'new' theatrical conventions. And, indeed, I'm sure people of a generation older than mine with real memories of music hall at the Alhambra and the Empire were far less shocked, although equally delighted by, *The Cheviot* . . . . But at least 7:84 did rediscover, revitalise and quite blatantly harness to their own purposes something which, if it had any right to be called 'a tradition', had been first bastardised and then allowed to atrophy. Impossible to remember just how fresh, how very cheeky indeed, seemed Bill Paterson's McChuckemup or Liz MacLennan's Harriet Beecher Stowe monologue or John Byrne's pop-up-book Heilan' set. Hard to recall how the unfamiliarity of hearing Dolina MacLennan's Gaelic songs and Alan Ross's fiddle

music swell to fill the Citizens' Theatre caused a shiver up the spine and a prickle at the back of the neck.

Dave Anderson must have absolutely loved *The Cheviot...* too. Because when I asked Dave MacLennan, "Hey, when did you and Anderson first get together?" He told me: "It was during 7:84's tour of "The Cheviot..." David and Tina were on honeymoon in Skye and they came to see it and that was it." "Love at first sight?" "Absolutely — he joined 7:84 for the next thing we did. Up until then Dave had been playing cabaret and piano in restaurants and bars, had been in bands in Canada, in London, and back in Scotland again." Dave Anderson was in many 7:84 shows like *Little Red Hen, My Pal and Me, The Game's a Bogey* and when he wrote, for *His Master's Voice* 7:84, it was directed by Dave MacLennan, so by the time they formed Wildcat together they were a formidable team.

Images from so many Wildcat shows crowd in, fragments of sound, scraps of lyric, rags of good-time riffs, eldritch and quite other-worldly notes of Terry Neason's. Like "Silent Town" ("The men and the women have nothing to *do*-ooo-oo"), where "there isn't a crush at the bathroom door/or a rush to be first down the stairs anymore/no gulping of coffee and Weetabix/no last minute panic, no piece to fix"; or "Cambusglen, the home of Rhythm and Blues" with its hellish pubs where "we'll just have a wee bit of order/Wan singer, wan song/no dancin'/no swearin'/no children/no denims/Wan singer, wan song/no politics/no religion/no catholics/no homos/no freedom/no progress/no nothin'/no danger". Or Terry again as the mother who has killed her child after hallucinating about a nuclear explosion she wishes to protect him from, in the classic, stark, courtroom-drama rock-opera *Any Minute Now* — ("all around Mary/carrion gather/black hoody crows/birds of a feather/even the white dove darkens her plumage/birds of a feather, together."). Or Terry singing "I'm leaving you" and Elaine C. Smith singing "Dead Liberty", the title song from the miners' strike show in 1984. Or Elaine's Mrs McGurk from *The Crack* belting out "Cry Me A River" ("They're cutting too much/and they're saving too much/they're shutting too much . . . they're not making too much contribution."), and her devastating pause before delivering the line that'll scupper, for once and for all, her daughter Tuesday's chance of a new dad for her illegitimate child, and how much it costs Mrs M. to give up on the wally and tell him "I hate Bezique, by the way." as she throws his sook-in present back in his face. Or Myra McFadyen bringing the house down with the "Mills-and-Boon-Doctor-Doctor" song from *Bedpan Alley*, "The Sister's Song" ("Isn't he great/isn't he fine/Don't you think he's so distinguished/He's just divine, wish he were mine/My love will not be extinguished/He sounds *So English*."). Or Myra the miner's wife, from *Dead Liberty* again, singing "What's the point in education?/You'll know all you need to know, you'll know a Mr You-Know-Who/They'll know, you know, that you're you-know-what/He'll know what he must do/Something old, something new, something borrowed, something blue", then the chorus "Cars going past on the motorway/People with somewhere to go/Traffic is fast on the motorway/By my window", which gave the most heartrending picture of Central Scotland loneliness and life-passing by I'd ever heard.

So it's just not true that Wildcat are obsessed with bits of warmed-over Americana. Well, not to the exclusion of doing some pretty ironic things with such pastiche material (and like all pastiche and parody it is in some ways an act of love.) Tam in *Heather Up Your Kilt* — as sung by Neil Hay — is forced to "God Bless America/For givin' us rhythm and blues/Keep your Dallas and your Dynasty/Your President, your foreign policy/I'll take Cagney and Lacey/Count Basie/Ray Charles/Even Spencer Tracey . . ." because "Don't talk to me about folk music/Don't talk to me about art/Don't talk to me about Andy Stewart/I know what I feel in my heart." David McNiven's "Presidential Waltz" does amazing and unexpected things to Country 'n' Western. Ditto for Gospel, in Anderson and MacLennan's "Babylon". ("And as sure as the wife of Lot was petrified right where she stood/You'll be turned into a pillar of salt if you worship Hollywood."). Scat, reggae, Dylanish folk rock, sweet fifties and sixties pop sung a-cappella, R and B, good old rock 'n' roll. Little Richard's legacy has taken root and is flourishing forever in the heart of Wildcat. Beautiful ballads. Outrageous send-ups of beautiful ballads from Rab Handleigh. The *It's a Free Country* company doing Gordon Dougall's "Bronchitis". The pure old fashioned music hall of Myra McFadyen's wee-boy-bursting in the factor's office scene in *Welcome To Paradise* — or of Rab Handleigh's heedrum-hodrum in the *Heather Up Your Kilt* song: ("Yir faither's up-a-'kye ma lad/ ma mither said wan day" or "The heilanman's umbrella/is ablow the Central Brig/an' ma hert

is in the studio/where they mak' Thingummyjig") . . . So many favourites . . . The sheer tuneful joy of Blythe Duff singing "All American Girl". Dave Anderson and Terry doing "My Big Brother" ("Ain't that just like the U.S.A/talking to the U.S.S.R/Ain't that just like the Soviets/talking to the U.S. of A") — and the wee girl of about thirteen or so I met in the queue for the lavatory after it, who was busy practising Dave Anderson's dance for that song, all the wee moves she could remember, "That baldy guy is absolutely brilliant by the way."

Well, so he is. So it's great that at long last there's a book of lyrics that will celebrate at least one strand of the work of Dave Anderson and Dave MacLennan. The companies of the various Wildcat shows over the years read like a Who's Who of Scottish Theatre, and others of us have had the chance to write for Wildcat — most notably David McNiven who wrote two shows solo and collaborated on many more. As Anderson and MacLennan get going on *Jotters* ("Our new show on education" — and the company's twenty-second —) it seems a good time to say here's to them, wha's like them?. More power to their scribbling elbows, tapping toes and ivory-tickling fingers.

Liz Lochhead

Liz Lochhead was born in Motherwell, but apart from spells in Canada and the USA, has lived most of her adult life in Glasgow. She is well known as a poet and performer of her own work and playwright for many Scottish Theatre Companies — including *Same Difference* for Wildcat. Her publications include Polygon bestsellers *Dreaming Frankenstein and Collected Poems* and *True Confessions*. Her acclaimed translation of *Tartuffe* published by Third Eye Centre / Polygon is also available.

THE WILDCAT'S PLAY AND PREY

Wildcat has now established itself as a highly popular company which in a series of tours has shown its fur, purr, and claws over most of Scotland. The touring, and the use of what have often been 'non-theatre' venues, have always been a part of their aim of reaching a working-class audience — an audience that might seldom go to the theatre except for music-hall, variety and pantomime. It is from traditions of music-hall and variety, farce and pantomime, that the company works, believing (rightly) that music is the great soldering-iron if you want to bring politics and entertainment together. As David Anderson said in an interview in *Radical Scotland* (No.19, Feb.-Mar.1986): "That's where I think we, Wildcat, are at our best, when it's like a Variety show but there's an argument there . . . an argument that develops, rather than a static situation." Some argument is necessary, both for the sake of drama and to avoid a sense of preaching to the converted. The subjects raised — unemployment, the miners' strike, the national health service, nuclear bases, multinational corporations, rich and poor, civil liberty, trade-union investments — are among the central and expected concerns of the Eighties, and Wildcat's challenge all along has been, to quote David MacLennan, "to reflect the struggles of our audience to protect themselves . . . in a way which helps them to carry on the fight." If music is the catalyst for doing this, the words of the songs or dialogue are obviously important and must be heard. And not only heard, but heard in a catchy and interesting way, with full reliance on swinging rhythm, frequent rhyme, and a fair dash of alliteration and other devices. The virtue of putting a selection of the songs in a book is to have a permanent record; the disadvantage is that the reader has to remember that without their music they have only half of their life: subtleties and ironies, as well as a more obvious emotional pointing or hilarious underlining, are inevitably lost.

Language too, nevertheless, makes its own points:

> "Should theatre be rhetorical
> Theological or empirical
> Paradoxical, metaphorical
> Or is one just a vehicle?"

> I had to say I'm into
> Agitation
> Propaganda
> Information
> Gimme candour
> Direct Action
> Disobedience
> Satisfaction
> Inconvenience
> Agitprop
> Over the top
> Political bop
> Don't ever stop
> Till they drop

("Beware the Poet")

If one has to "beware the poet", with his perhaps rhetorical or self-indulgent or style-centred art, the warning itself pays tribute to the rhetoric of the stylistic contrast between question and answer and of the five-rhyme climax. Like any poet, the song-writers revel in the language they use, and enjoy particularly an inventive and opportunistic proliferation of rhyme, which serves both as mnemonic for singers and as a ready marker for the ears of a popular audience to catch. Or again, a strongly defined rhythm, whether it originates in the music or the lyric or both equally, can be used in various highly suggestive ways to draw the listener into a context, a world, very different from (but always to be related to) that of contemporary politics. Biblical chants and spirituals might seem to loom large in "Babylon", as indeed the title implies:

> And they worshipped Egypt and they worshipped Athens
>   and they worshipped Rome
> And they worshipped Steeple and they worshipped Tower
>   and they worshipped Dome
> And they worshipped Cup and they worshipped Candle
>   and they worshipped Wine
> And they worshipped Symbol and they worshipped Image
>   and they worshipped Sign

The repeated triads, the full rhymes, and the clarity of the analysis if we want to think about it (the succession of increasingly rarefied delusions — worship of the national state, of its religion, of the ritual objects of that religion, and finally of the symbolic status of these objects) are conveyed

3

through a menacing rhythm which suggests something more primitive than analytic. So what is Babylon? We are brought back nearer home:

> The Devil's disciple
> is alienation
> of people from people
> of mind from emotion
> of man from the temple
> of his own creation
> of the slum from the castle
> we call this situation
> Babylon

And in "Glasgow Song", whether deliberately or accidentally (happy accident if the latter), the long-lined metre of Tennyson's "Locksley Hall" is used, as it was by Tennyson, to lay out historical and prophetic vistas.

All this is no more than to say that the Wildcat songs have an accomplished variety and range of approach, and that it would be wrong to see them *merely* as vehicles for political, economic, and social ideas. They *are* that, obviously, and Wildcat's purpose, as far as their whole deployment of music, lyrics, and dialogue is concerned, has been to develop a 'language' that a popular and largely working-class audience will accept and enjoy. The content also had to be acceptable, though its appeal could still be fresh, with challenging and unexpected moments. In the interview mentioned above, David Anderson said that he was 'reflecting' rather than 'pioneering' the political thinking of his audiences, and that even that was difficult enough. "It's hard enough to decide where the politics end and where the entertainment begins; we don't think there's a certainty about that line. Either you think politics is entertaining or entertainment is political." In fact they manage the mix extremely well (the occasional flogging of a moribund horse, or throwing a baby out with the bathwater, can be put down to over-enthusiasm), and that is no doubt the reason for their success with the public. They satirize with gusto where they know their audience will be with them ("Knightsbridge is Nice"), but they are not afraid to throw spanners in the works (the confrontation between redundant worker and Union Man in "Blootered"), and some of their most interesting points are made through the mouth of an offbeat but significant character, like the disturbed Davey Galbraith of "Davey Galbraith's Rant",

who has found no satisfaction in either soldiering or panel-beating and wants to give the Labour movement a MacDiarmidesque push which it claims not to understand:

> I wanted life
> in massive doses
> I wanted bread
> but I wanted roses
> And what did I get?
> I got mair pay and better hours
> but no hope and no flowers
> and no answer and no solution
> no holy grail
> no revolution
> Scotland sitting on its arse
> acting out an ancient farce
> "Galbraith, you're on your own"
> they said
> "You've lost the place
> you're off your head"

Occasionally a period of pause, of atmosphere, of elegy, will sum up in a more lyrical way a good deal of what the plays are saying, about the human waste of a grasping, ill-run society, as in "Silent Town". The long-term unemployed have no rush to rise early:

> When morning's old
> the curtains draw
> in the streets of Silent Town
> and air is cold
> and wind is raw
> in a flimsy dressing gown.
> No need to make haste
> there's the afternoon
> it's a waste of your time
> if you finish too soon.

When they pull the stops out, Wildcat can be very rousing. The final song in *Heather Up Your Kilt*, "The Right of Nations", has a message for American nuclear imperialism, and indirectly for the London government which props and underwrites that imperialism, to the effect that "You say you're bringing business, but you're shutting down the place". The installations must go. And there is a neat echo of the Americans' own "No taxation without representation", when they were casting off the British yoke, in the concluding chorus, which is highly effective in the theatre — and true too.

> The right of nations
> To self-determination
> The right of nations
> To self-determination
> No more confrontation
> And militarization
> Ecological pollution
> It's a practical solution
> The right of nations
> To self-determination

Edwin Morgan

Edwin Morgan was born in Glasgow in 1920. Was Titular Professor of English at Glasgow University until 1980. Poetry-reading tours in U.S., Czechoslovakia, Hungary, Turkey. Librettos for opera and music-theatre. Books include: *Poems of Thirty Years* (1982), *Sonnets from Scotland* (1984), *Selected Poems* (1985), *From the Video Box* (1986), *Newspoems* (1987).

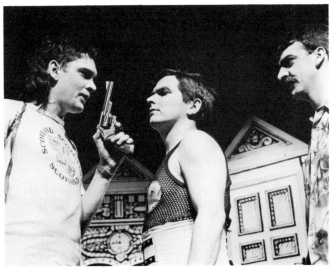

Rab Handleigh, Gordon Dougall and Steven Wren
in *Heather up your Kilt*
Photo Alan Wylie

David Hicks
in *The Painted Bird*
Photo George Oliver

5

THE PAINTED BIRD

Wildcat's first show opened at the McLellan Galleries in Sauchiehall Street, Glasgow on 14 September 1978. The variety of venues we played with our first production set the pattern for later tours. There were gigs in Easterhouse Community Centre, The Star Social Club, Strontian Village Hall, Whitburn Miners' Welfare, Aberdeen Arts Centre and Dundee Rep. Altogether we did 37 performances in 28 venues from Brora to Barrhead.

The hero of the piece was Davey Galbraith, a Panel Beater, "A clocker in/a knocker out/of dunts and shunts/in the backs and fronts/of corporation buses". Davey was a manic depressive and became a victim of that cure-all treatment for the mentally disordered — the pharmaceutical sandbag.

It is interesting, in retrospect, that we should have chosen to look at the treatment of the mentally ill in Britain at a time when the English electorate were poised to commit their greatest ever act of collective insanity and vote for Margaret Thatcher.

David McNiven, who was to collaborate with us on many successful productions, gave a most sensitive performance as Davey Galbraith, and Mary Brennan, writing in the *Glasgow Herald*, thought the show was "One of the most hopeful omens for Scotland's theatrical future." In making this prediction she placed herself alongside the Delphic Oracle and the Brahan Seer in the accuracy of her prophecy!

THINGMY

I woke up this morning
full of the joys of thingmy.
There wasn't a cloud on the ceiling.
I felt I could fly like a budgie.
My heart was alive with the songs
that they play on the do-da.
Its hard to explain how I'm feeling.
I hummed a wee tune on the cludgie.
I slid down the bannister.
I'm Fred Astaire
I'm your dancing lodger
Ginger Rogers!

I came into breakfast.
Go to my work on a whatsit.
Magnificent value of milk.
I couldn't tell Stork from the butter.
My mind was aspin with the thrill
of my work and etcetera.
My sow's ear has turned into silk.
I'm off to the job in a flutter.
I'm riding a hackney cab.
I'm Alan Ladd
I'm the pride of labour
Zsa Zsa Gabor!

Oh it's magic
Oh it's great
Transportation of the Welfare State
You must study
You must toil
I'm on vacation and I can't be late.

Who wouldn't be happy?
A life that's so whatdyamacallit.
A life that's so thingmybob.
A life that's so what can you say?
A life that's so full of God knows
where we ought to begin.
I can't wait to get to my job.
Every day is a wonderful day.
I'm completely delirious
I'm serious
I'm your sole supporter
John Travolta!

Oh it's magic
Oh it's great
Transportation of the Welfare State
You must study
You must toil
I'm on vacation and I can't be late.

NEIGHBOUR'S SONG

Her man, have you heard?
He's away with the birds.
Can't tell cheese from chalk.
It's the talk of the block.

Just think of the disgrace
If your man lost the place . . .
Everybody knows he's aff his heid.

Tittle tat Tittle tat Tittle tat
Tattle tit Tattle tit Tattle tit
Fancy that Fancy that Fancy that.
            Is that no sad?

What a shame What a shame What a shame
So it is So it is So it is
In the name In the name In the name
            What a business!

He's as nutty as a fruitcake
He is madder than a hatter
Daft as a brush he's got watter
            On the brain
            What a shame
            What a business!

CONFORMING

Working to keep your
Head above water
Good little housewife
Just like they taught you
No thoughts of living
Laughing and lusting
Just of the washing
Cleaning and dusting
            That's right

Conforming Conforming Conforming
Performing Performing Performing
Your Duty Your Duty Your Duty
            That's right

Working to keep your
Man like a motor
Fed for the morning
Fit for the slaughter
Too tired for living
Joking and talking
Spending an evening
Going out walking
            That's right

Conforming Conforming Conforming
Performing Performing Performing
Your Duty Your Duty Your Duty
            That's right

DAVEY GALBRAITH'S RANT

God? aye — I used to believe in him
like a fool
what they taught at school
how the pearly gates
would open wide
and lose or win
we would all ride in
in spite of original sin
an' that
but I smelled a rat
was it no' just a way to say
OK?
that anything goes
God knows but he doesnae care
"The perfect creed for greed!"
cried the rich man
riding the camel
through the eye of the needle
so I left the church
in the lurch
and I left my school
and went in search
of heaven on earth
but I found a dearth
of angels
hingin' frae Bridgeton Cross
a cross that I had to bear
it was there
you see
that I got my start
in the noble art
of panel beating
a chance meeting
wi' a pal frae school
and yours truly
intae a trade —
made!
one day
a young apprentice
next day
National Service
ah well to hell
travel excitement romance
and a chance

to meet the officer class
at last
me a sentry
rubbing shou'ders wi' the gentry
who had lunch
instead of dinner
and had dinner
for their tea
perhaps they held the key
life you see
had become a quest
I couldn't rest
till I found my holy grail
in fact what I got
was Aldershot
and a lot of rot
from a daft major
who thought that Scotland
was a village
north of
Watford Junction
and the function
of the army
was to keep it there
to keep the Russians in their place
police the human race
and show a face
in Cyprus, Kenya and Hong Kong
and right or wrong
the merchant banks
said thanks
the major joined the ranks
of the city
and Supermac
made the witty crack
"You've never had it so good"
so back I went to civvy street
though none the wiser
and became an early riser
a clocker in
and knocker out
of dunts and shunts
in the backs and fronts
of Corporation buses

8

hard slog
but me a cog
a working part
in the heart of the labour movement
a small improvement
you could say
on Forces pay
and barrack squares
and the same old prayers
of the regiment's
Charlie Chaplin
and then it started happenin'
a new season
a new sensation
a revelation
a new solution
a revolution
politics spelt with a labour 'p'
it had to be
the way for me
for one and all
to have a ball
to smash the walls
to set us free
and let us be
ourselves!
the answer!
don't get me wrong
I didn't want to burn or bomb
or start a flood of blood
in Newton Mearns or Eaglesham
I wanted life
in massive doses
I wanted bread
but I wanted roses
and what did I get?
I got mair pay and better hours
but no hope and no flowers
and no answer and no solution
no holy grail
no revolution
Scotland sitting on its arse
acting out an ancient farce
'Galbraith, you're on your own'

they said
'You've lost the place
you're off your head'
and so I am
and proud and glad
to lose the place
in a world that's mad.

DON'T KNOW

I don't know if I'm sleeping
I don't know if I'm dreaming
Lying in the dark and hearing him
Pacing round the hall
I don't know if he's weeping
I don't know if he's scheming
Crying in the dark and fearing him
Facing to the wall.

I don't know how much more I can take
Saying that it's all right but I
Don't know why I'm trying to pretend.

I spend my days in hoping
I spend my days in thinking
Thinking of the times we used to spend
Years so long ago
I spend my days in coping
I spend my days in sinking
Sinking at the thought where-will-it-end?
Fears so strong I know

I don't know how much more I can take
Saying that it's all right but I
Don't know why I'm trying to pretend.

G.P.'s SONG

When I was a young man and newly qualified
Diseases were infectious, you caught them and you died.
Diphtheria and Typhoid were the scourges of the day
They crept like shadows thro' the slums
       and carried you away.
It was relatively simple to treat wee Johnny's pimple
And poultice aching backs for Granny Macs
When I was a young man.

When I was a young man discoveries were sought.
Viruses were fallible, diseases could be fought.
Bacterial infection took a dose of penicillin
A posterior injection, pop a pill in, send my bill in . . .
There was mass inoculation for protection of the nation
And milk and orange juice to keep you spruce
When I was a young man.

Now I am an old man I find that more and more
There's a different kind of patient who
      is knocking at my door.
I can cope with halitosis, give them doses for their noses
But my certain diagnosis of the way the story goes is
That the new tuberculosis is psychoses and neuroses
Epidemics of diphtheria replaced by mass hysteria
Influenza and the cholics can't compete with alcoholics
Broken bones at least have flesh on
Can you plaster a depression?

Next please.

GET OUT OF MY WAY

I met a painter without any pictures
I met a poet without any words
I heard a teacher without any learning
I heard a singer without any tune
I saw a landscape without any features
I saw a country without any birds
I met a preacher without any sermon
I met two lovers without a moon in June

I see a person without aspirations
I see a man who's no longer a man
I see him robbed of his will to be human
I see him stripped of what made him unique
I see no pity in his situation
I see the victim must carry the can
I see no chance of there being a new man
He's the living proof that cursed are the meek

What could he have done
They could not forgive?
He could not be left alone
           To live
What could be his crime
They could not allow?
He must be a threat but why
           And how?

Like a painted bird
They have clipped his wings
Locked him in a cage his legs
           In rings

When they let him go
They will rest assured
He will fly no more they'll say
           He's cured

I'm gonna hassle till I get some answers
I'm gonna crowd them till I know the score
I'm gonna find them and sort out the chancers
I'm gonna show them they've trouble in store

Are you with me or are you against me?
'It's not my fault' can I hear you say?
Are you the answer or part of the problem?
If that's what you are
Then get out of my way.

THE COMPLETE HISTORY OF ROCK 'N' ROLL

In this show Wildcat traced the history of Rock 'n' Roll right back to its origins in Partick. Kenny Dunlop and Alex Semple were the band in the Cambusglen Miners' Welfare. For Kenny, Rock was nothing to do with what happened on the Mississippi Delta — it was to do with a one and threepenny ticket to the Gods in the Glasgow Empire one Friday night in the late nineteen fifties. For Alex, it went back to Govanhill; "Grandpa plays the songs he knows, from Minstrel shows, and G.H. Elliot, we huvnae got a telly, — it disnae matter." The show opened in Glasgow, in Third Eye Centre's Main Gallery and the audience seemed to know what Alex and Kenny were talking about.

Wildcat had not yet built a mass audience and after a small house in the Civic Theatre in Ayr, the Ayrshire Post carried the headline, "And you dumbos missed it." Thus began a long and friendly relationship with the local press which was not so much the case with the nationals. They were beginning to ask, ". . . but is it art?"

While some have tried to answer this question we have tried to answer the question put by one of the characters in the play, "What kind of music do the *folk* sing in their baths?"

Andy Park at Radio Clyde broadcast the whole show as their first full length radio drama.

David McNiven
in *The Complete History of Rock 'N' Roll*
Photo George Oliver

FAMILY LIFE

Here we are in Govanhill
with Uncle Bill
and Uncle Harry
We're as happy as Larry
So we are
Granpa plays the songs he knows
From minstrel shows
And G.H. Elliott
We huvnae got a telly — it
Disnae matter.

Uncle Frank is a baritone
Ma Daddy is a tenor
Harry sings like a sousaphone and
Me! Ah'm no even a fiver.

Granpa went to work when he was only twelve years old
But the family sticks together
At the crack of dawn he went out in the rain and cold
But the family sticks together
He was only seventeen when he was sent to war
But the family sticks together
And still he doesn't know what he was fighting for
But the family sticks together
He saw depression in the twenties
Recession in the thirties
And through every generation
There's been sickness and starvation
But the family sticks together
Thank God we've got each other.

It's been poverty and war and work your life away
But the family sticks together
And it's been wonderin' if the people will be free someday
But the family sticks together
It's been strugglin' just to keep your wife and kids alive
But the family sticks together
It's a wonder that the workin' people still survive
But the family sticks together
From the father to the son
So the family will run

Be respectful to your mother
And protective of your brother
So the family sticks together
Thank God we've got each other.

Family life
Family life
Makes all the trouble and strife
So much easier to bear
Thank God for
Family life.

KITCHEN

All the women pitch in
Workin' in the kitchen
Makin' up the pieces
For the nephews and nieces
In nineteen fifty.

Tryin' to be happy
Washing out the nappies
Makin' do and mending
All the time it's never ending
Be wise be thrifty.

You would think a Sunday
Ought to be the one day
You could stop the clatter
Take a rest and have a natter
Wouldn't that be nifty?
It's true what they say
A woman's work is never done
in nineteen fifty.

Family life,
Family life
Be a good mother,
Be a good wife,
And love the children that you bear
That's family life.

BABY

Here you are in Govanhill
With Auntie Jill
And Auntie Netta
You're jist gonnae get a
Trolley hame.
You're a right wee beauty too
It's your duty to
Grow up and marry
Somebody like Uncle Harry
Whit a shame.

Family life
Is the only life
It keeps us all together
You'll have weans and you'll be a wife
Like your granny
And your mother.

Family life
Family life
Be a good mother
Be a good wife
It won't be long before it's gone
Thank God for
Family life.

With your brothers
All the others
All together
For each other
Won't be long before it's gone
Family life.

THE CHAPTER

Here we are in '56
We're at the flicks
Tae see Tom Mix
Look out, he's comin' up behind ye!
Don't miss next week's exciting chapter.

Ah wish Ah wis
like Buster Crabbe
Ah think he's fab
He's got a stetson
You can put your bets on
He's the fastest.

We walk home wi' the bowly legs
And kid on we are cowdies
Gies a drag of your single fag
Make it we're the Goodies
And youse are the Baddies.

The Company
in *The Complete History of Rock 'N' Roll*
Photo George Oliver

"WAN SINGER"

Youse all know me, I'm Harry McDade
Through the week I'm a plumber to trade
'Til the weekend when I've got it made —
I'm a singer.
Youse are here for the crack and the booze
We don't have any darkies or jews
And youse'll get barred if any of youse
Goes your dinger.

DUMMIES

Wan singer, wan song
No dancin'
No swearin'
No children
No denims
Wan singer, wan song.

Efter a' the work youse have done
Youse deserve a wee bit of fun
But we'll hae none of last week's carry oan —
It was murder.
Youse are here for to set yourselves free
That's the gemme; it's O.K. by me
But if youse don't mind, we'll jist have a wee
Bit of order.

Wan singer, wan song
No politics
No religion
No catholics
No homos
Wan singer, wan song.

We've got music
And we've got booze
We've got cabaret
And we've got booze
We've got bingo
And we've got booze
At the welfare

Wan singer, wan song
No freedom
No progress
No nothin'
No danger
Wan singer, wan song.

We premièred this piece in Cumbernauld's new Cottage Theatre the week before it was officially opened by the equally new Under Secretary of State for Scotland, Malcolm Rifkind MP. We have attempted to dog his footsteps and those of his boss ever since.

Dummies was a dossers' eye view of Thatcher's Britain — a society from which they did not expect to derive a great deal of benefit. The show owed something to Brecht but more to Kurt Weill and it contained within it the seeds of a style of 'Beggars' Cabaret' which we were to return to from time to time.

We took the production to the Project Theatre in Dublin, our first trip out of Scotland, where it was warmly received. Was this because real beggars plied O'Connell Street and the Dubliners could easily see the same shame on the community developing across the water?

The critic of *The Irish Times* said that he would pay to hear Terry Neason sing a telephone directory in Gregorian plain chant, which was a widely held view at the time and still is, albeit a slightly depressing one, for the writer of lyrics.

The Company
in *Dummies*
Photo George Oliver

David Anderson and Terry Neason
in *Dummies*
Photo George Oliver

BABYLON

It says in the Bible
That civilisation
Is destined to crumble
From disintegration
The Tower of Babel
The same as our nation
Fell down into rubble
With rotten foundations
And the truth of the fable
Has a realisation —

Babylon!

In the last days
Men will be
According to the Book of Timothy
Vain, proud, lovers of money
Swollen with conceit.
They'll be arrogant, egotist
Profligate, hypocrites
Faithless
Lovers of pleasure
Liars, thieves and cheats.

It says in the Bible
In the Book of Revelations
The eternal apostle
In all generations
Brings portents of trouble
Whatever the nation
The message is simple
Needs no explanation
The Devil's disciple
Is alienation
Of people from people
Of mind from emotion
Of man from the temple
Of his own creation
Of the slum from the castle
We call this situation

Babylon!

Brothers and sisters
              Yes, Lord
In the congregation
              Here, tonight
Let me tell you a story
              Yes, Yes
Of the Dawn of Creation
              Lord, Lord

In the Garden of Eden
When the world was young
They lived in holy harmony
With no space between
The man and the woman and
The earth and the sky and the sea

Then along came the serpent and he tempted Eve
              Save us, Save us
Taste the Tree of Life taste the good and evil
              That's a sin, That's a sin
And Adam ate the apple and you'd better believe
              We do, We do
That they saw they were naked and believed in the devil
              Bad news, Bad news
Now this ain't nothin' but a metaphor
              Metaphor, Metaphor
Writ down by the wise men in the days of yore
              Days of yore, Days of yore
False prophets told the people that it came to pass
              Came to pass, Came to pass
Now they teach it in the churches with the fancy glass
              Fancy glass, Fancy glass

So the people were told they were born in sin
   by the Scribes and the Pharisees.
They forgot they were born in the image of God
   and they fell down on their knees.

And they worshipped Gold and they worshipped Silver
  and they worshipped Jewels.
And they worshipped Kings and they worshipped Goats
  and they worshipped Bulls.
And they worshipped Egypt and they worshipped Athens
  and they worshipped Rome.
And they worshipped Steeple and they worshipped Tower
  and they worshipped Dome.
And they worshipped Cup and they worshipped Candle
  and they worshipped Wine.
And they worshipped Symbol and they worshipped Image
  and they worshipped Sign.
And they kissed the ground where the hero walked
  where the idol stood.

And they all fell down
Right to the ground
And they trembled at the sound
Of the Voice of the mortal
At the earthly portal
Of the Palace of Adonis
And Narcissus
And libidinous
Licentiousness!
And as sure as the Wife of Lot was petrified
  right where she stood
You'll be turned into a pillar of salt if you
  worship Hollywood.

NOBODY

A quiet life
a nobody
a place to be
a stowaway
a quiet life
a little peace
a chance to be
anonymous

It's an easy life
for nobody
It's hard to be
a somebody
but nobody
can bother me
as long as I
am nobody

Seems like everybody but me
is lookin' for somebody to be
but me I just want to be
nobody

Just call me Joe
that'll do
you'll never know
if it's true
it's easier
not to say
nothin' much
I'm nobody
I tried it once
I gave it up
it didn't work
it never does
for somebody
must take the blame
they say to me
"What's your name"

Seems like everybody but me
is lookin' for somebody to be
but me I just want to be
nobody

Born to be a
nobody
there's nobody
in my family
we had no name
no claim to fame
everybody
was a nobody
and everybody knew
except me, except me

I used to think
foolish boy when I did not know
I could grow like you're supposed to grow
I could grow any way I choose
cocky kid in my baby shoes
no ass in my home-made trews
that was long before I got the news
about the big stick

I used to be
so proud I was ten feet tall
get up and do it again if I had a fall
I was gonna do what I wanted to
find out if the truth was true
grab hold of my proper due
this was all long before I knew
about the big stick
they hit you with
when you step out of line

The doorman at the cinema
    when ye tried to jump the queue.
the woman in the corner shop
    when ye nicked a penny chew
the Janny in the playground
    when ye got into a fight
the teacher in the classroom
    when ye didny get it right
the polis when he came around
    tae see yer da at night
with the big stick

Just call me Joe
that'll do
you'll never know
if it's true
it's easier
not to say
nothin' much
I'm nobody

Seems like everybody but me
is lookin' for somebody to be
but me I just want to be
nobody

THE DUMMIES' SONG

In a forest that is petrified
Stand the statues of the idolised
Watched by people who are mummified
In a world that's been immobilised.

By the way by the Clyde
Thousands more on the dole   nothing changes
Factories closing down   nothing changes
Closing yards, closing schools   nothing changes
Cutting this, cutting that   nothing changes
Prices soar, wages freeze   nothing changes
   nothing changes.

When you stroll in the city
When you see the old beggar
Do you think, 'What's his future?'
And forget that he's living
Here and now just like you in the present?
Hanging round waiting for something pleasant
Bunch of flowers, suit of clothes, brace of pheasant
While you wait for the change for the better,
For the jam on your thin bread and butter,
You could end up like him in the gutter.

Will your savings protect you?
Is your home like a castle?
Do you carry insurance?
Have you shares in the market?
Can you cope with the rate of inflation?
Are you safe in your own occupation?
Are you sure of a watch and a pension?
We agree, you and me, for protection
Nothing beats having cash, it's perfection.
But a slump or a crash doesn't bear reflection.

You can't hold the tide at bay,
You can blossom or decay,
You can grow or mould away,
Life won't wait a single day.
You can't wait on luck or fate,
You can't take a rest or break,
You can't pause to take a breath,
You can't put off life or death.

You can join in our ranks in the morning,
You can be just like us with no warning,
Simple truth, fact of life, no adorning!

We were once all like you, we had daddies
Uncle Bills, Auntie Flos, and our mummies.
Still we're all just like you now,
                    we're battered dummies.

Take a tip from the dossers
Spanner Joe and the Reverend
Mrs. M. Nettie Curtains.
Each of us hit the skids and we're certain
If you don't change the world, it'll change you,
Pick you up, throw you out or exchange you,
Pass you by, crucify or derange you.
Are you sure you're so pure that you won't slide
down the hill to a bench on the Clydeside?
You could fall one and all like a landslide.

BLOOTER

When we first talked of doing a show about unemployment
and the new technology in December 1979, there were
1,355,500 people out of work. When we opened *Blooter* at
the Edinburgh Festival the following August, the figure had
reached two million.

There was something sadly ironic about the arrival of
silicon chips. Not only did they control the operations of the
robots which were taking over the jobs of mere mortals, but
they also provided the 'intelligence' of the ubiquitous space
invader machines which were relieving increasingly large
numbers of unemployed punters of their hard earned giros.
Blootered at work by the boss and blootered in the pub by
aliens from outer space.

In the course of researching for this show the whole
Company became addicted to playing Space Invaders,
Asteroids and all the other variations on the theme of "A
fool and his money are easily parted."

As we toured the large urban housing schemes with this
production, we saw more and more of the silent towns and
the human wastage brought about by the religious fervour
of monetarism.

Alan Tall
in *Blooter*
Photo Antonia Reeve

FUN FUN FUN FUN

When you drop
into your local
for a pint a nip a natter
can you hear
your neighbour's patter
over all the noise and clatter

You can play
the one arm bandit
hand it over Thursday's wages
you can join
the row of lemons
demonstrate your skill for ages

       Fun, fun, fun, fun

You can gawp
at colour telly
skelly-eyed till closing time
you can drink
in Larry Grayson
chase 'im down with gin and lime

you can watch
the go-go dancer
prance her way across the floor
you can see the lunchtime stripper
slip her bra – hey give us more

       Fun, fun, fun, fun

You can hear
the latest goldie
oldie hit or juke box disco
ten pence buys
the sound of Tamla-
Motown-Nashville-San-Francisco

       Fun, fun, fun, fun

DUET FOR A DATE

Goin' for a date
    Hope he won't forget
Better not be late
    Hope he won't regret
Hope she's in the mood
    Hope he's on his way
Hope she's feelin' good
    Hope I look O.K.

Hope it all goes alright
It's tonight. It's tonight.

    Better do the face
    Better do the hair
    Better make a choice
    What I'm gonna wear
    Ladder in my tights
    Broke another nail
    Spilled a jar of cream
    God I'm looking pale

    What a mess, I'm a fright
    It's tonight. It's tonight.

Better have a shave
Razor's getting old
Better take a shower
Water's running cold
Lashing on the Brut
Stinging like a bee
Better press the suit
Where the hell's my key?

Got my fags, got my lights
It's tonight. It's tonight.

Girls meets boy meets
Girl by chance
Office party
At a dance
Watchin' movies
In the stalls
West Side Story
Guys 'n Dolls

Settle down
Cue the sound
Cue the lights
It's tonight.

Take her for a drink?
Take her to a show?
Hell I'd better think
Where we're gonna go

Couldn't give a damn
What we're gonna do
Long as we're alone
For an hour or two

Hope it all goes alright
It's tonight. It's tonight.

BLOOTERED

The search is on for Mister Brown.
He hurries out to search the town!
No stone unturned however small.
His bridge is burned, he's heard the call.
Find out the score! Reveal the lie!
There's more to this than meets the eye!
Oh! His search began with the Union Man . . .
        Brother!
        Comrade
        Welcome
        hell, come on
        come in
        excuse the mess
        the Press,
        you know
        were here.
        A beer?
                        No thanks.
                        No beer.
                        Not now.

Not now?
Well how can I help
and what can I do?
                It's the buroo!
                I've joined the ranks
                of the unemployed,
                and I'm annoyed
                'cos I've paid my dues
                to the likes of youse
                year in
                year out.
No need to shout!
Just hold it there!
Your dues
you say?
                Aye! Why?
                Just why the hell?
I'll tell you why.
They go to swell
your pension fund.
Your pension
not to mention
all the other benefits . . .
                Benefits,
                crap!
                I'm on the dole!
The whole world is!
Or will be soon.
You want the moon,
the sun
the stars!
We do our best . . .
                I'm not impressed
The Union tries
                You compromise!
OK, wise guy,
you know the score.
What else, what more,
can the Union do?
                You're asking me?
I'm telling you!
We haven't gotta
choice . . .

There speaks the voice
of the leadership.
Look!
Get a grip,
you're years behind.
You talk and talk,
they close the shop!
Negotiate?
They lock the gate!
You're out of date.
They're years ahead.
Percentages.
Manning.
Differentials
— inessentials!
They're in control.
We're on the dole!
The Union's role
has never been
political.
You're critical,
but that's the way.
You pay your dues,
we fight for you.
But when you're out
there's nowt
that we can do.
That's when you know that you've been
blootered!
Neutered
by someone who's astuter than you.
You'll boo-hoo
but
what'll you do?
Hee-Haw?
Surely naw!
There's no law
says its got to be.

And when you find that you've been
snookered
pressure-cookered
in the micro-wave
who is gonna save you?
Who, indeed?
Don't you see that you need
all the other fish in the sea?
They take your gold and give you pewter.
They think they're cuter than you.
They've got you on a skewer.
But they're fewer than you!
Why not take a crack,
counter-attack,
blooter them back?
                    Ah! I see, it's the Union . . .
No! You've been blootered!
Ask the stockbroker
what he did with your
pension fund.
The Fund?
Ah, yes . . .
Now let me see . . .
where will it be?
We deal with
three
or four
or more,
invest them soundly
here and there in
stocks and shares,
blue chips,
gilt edge
to hedge
against inflation.
Curse of the nation!
                    It's information
                    that I'm after.
                    Facts. — You know?
                    Like where did
                    my money go?

Quite so, quite so . . .
Well, I'll be frank,
we sank a bit
in Barclays Bank
Johannesburg . . .
a lovely town,
my cousin's there . . .
now where was I?
                    In Barclays Bank
Why thank you! Yes!
Then, at a guess,
there's some in land,
in real estate,
greatest of stuff
can't get enough,
then property
and industry . . .
                    The Union's into
                    all of that?
                    Away and —
Quite!
And other things
besides.
In works of Art
and precious stones
and foreign loans,
let's make no bones,
they want a good
return!
And, for my fee,
I see they do.
                    Oh, thanks a bunch!
Well, off to lunch.
Glad I could help!
                    Don't mention it,
                    thanks.
Oh!
I nearly forgot.
A fair bit goes
to the merchant banks.
That's when you know
that you've been blootered . . .

Ah! I see — it's money!
No, no, you've been blootered.
Ask the merchant banker
what he did with your contributions.
        We put together
        packages,
        enormous deals,
        and oil the wheels
        of international
        commerce,
        financing schemes
        with expertise
        for Japanese
        exporters . . .
                    Support your town
                    and wear their colours?
The nation state
is out of date.
We've gone worldwide,
swum with the tide.
Tractors for Zambia,
a dam in Gambia,
weapons for Oman,
whisky for Amin . . .
                    I thought he'd gone?
Upon my word
he has — you're right!
A flight of Phantoms
for a Sheik,
a British week
in Pakistan,
a "cracker" plant
in Venezuela
you know . . .
the paraphenalia
of international trade!
                    Paid for
                    with my dues?
Well, those
and a million other
odds and ends,
we blend together
from here and there.

What's your latest
fancy notion?
We've set in motion,
just since you ask,
a Belgrade plant —
Barron UK!
to manufacture
Space Marauders
behind the Iron Curtain.
Barrons!
Are you certain?
You mean to say
I've helped to pay for that?!!
Finally I get it. It's the new technology
— the silicon chip.
No! no! no! There's nothing wrong with any of that!
It's not what you do,
it's the way that they do it —
That's when you know
that you've been blootered.
That's when you know
that you've been blootered.

David Hicks, Angie Rew and David McNiven
in *Blooter*
Photo Antonia Reeve

SILENT TOWN

When daylight breaks
The buses purr
Through the streets of Silent Town
But no-one wakes
And no-one stirs
From their cosy eiderdown.
There isn't a crush
At the bathroom door
Or a rush to be first
Down the stairs anymore,
No gulping of coffee and Weetabix,
No last minute panic, no piece to fix.
The pavement's deserted,
No bus stop queue,
For the men and the women
Have nothing to do.
No, the men and the women
Have nothing to do.

When morning's old
The curtains draw
In the streets of Silent Town
And air is cold
And wind is raw
In a flimsy dressing gown.
No need to make haste
There's the afternoon
It's a waste of your time
If you finish too soon.
No letters to answer, no bills to pay
Well, none that won't keep to another day.
The paper's unopened
'Cos nothing is new
And the men and the women
Have nothing to do.
No, the men and the women
Have nothing to do.

Terry Neason and Billy Johnstone
in *Blooter*   Photo Antonia Reeve

The wasted hours
And wasted days
Grow into wasted years.
A wasted life
Three score and ten
When the ferryman appears.
Cast off the rope,
Abandon all hope
All ye who enter here.

It's four o'clock
And walk the dog
Through the streets of Silent Town.
And darn a sock
And fetch a log
'Cos the fire is dying down.
'No nobody came
But it's early yet
It's a shame I agree
Don't you worry, my pet!
No visits, surprises, no nothing, dear
No, we're just on our own my love I fear
Then lapse into silence
'Cos nothing is new
When the men and the women
Have nothing to do.
No, the men and the women
Have nothing to do.

It's night at last
So draw the blinds
On the streets of Silent Town.
A day has passed
And no-one minds
In their cosy eiderdown.
They've wound up the clocks
On the kitchen walls
And the locks are all on
On the doors in the halls
And silence unbroken and nothing said
Is everyone sleeping or are they dead?
The paper's unopened
'Cos nothing is new
And the men and the women
Had nothing to do.
No, the men and the women
Had nothing to do.

THE LAST TOAST

Let us raise our glasses full of sparkling wine
Let us join together in a toast
Compliment the hostess on the way we dine
Compliment the carver on the roast
Work of art done in oils

Here's to the winners
Regrets to the losers
Here's to successes
Forget all the failures
Here's to the victory
And here's to the spoils

Let us raise our glasses to our enterprise
Let us drink together to our kind
Celebrate the winning celebrate the prize
Celebrate the way we wined and dined
And we won by our toils

Let us raise our glasses with a grateful sigh
Here's to one more round against the odds
Yet another crisis we have overcome
One more dedication to the Gods
Hoist the flag, hoist the royals

Squeezed like a lemon
Tell me is it
An acquired taste?
Must be bitter.
So exquisite
Tell me is it laced?
With the acid is it sour?
Can you bear it?
Is your stomach lined?
Don't you care, don't you mind?

Here's to the winners
Regrets to the losers
Here's to successes
Forget all the failures
Here's to the victory
And here's to the wine
And we've made up our mind

David McNiven, Angie Rew
and David Hicks in *Blooter*   Photo Antonia Reeve

They take your gold and give you pewter
They think they're cuter than you
They've got you on a skewer
But they're fewer than you
Why not do your duty
Bloot or be Blootered
Don't be left behind
Make up your mind

Will you ride
With the hunter
Or flee with the fox?
Will you soar
Like the falcon
Or hide in the rocks?

When the bugle blares
And the trumpet sounds
Will you run with the hares?
Will you hunt with the hounds?
Will you run with the hares?
Will you hunt with the hounds?
Will you sit on the fence
And pretend to be blind?
Will you make up your mind?

CONFESSIN' THE BLUES

"It was Karl Marx who said 'The first division of labour is between man and woman for child bearing . . . and the first class oppression that of the female sex by the male.'" *The Jewish Echo* offered this quote as a suitable introduction to *Confessin' the Blues*, so you will not be surprised to learn we were invited to perform it at the home of the Berliner Ensemble in the G.D.R. One week in East Berlin, the next week in East Kilbride.

The show's heroine was Fiona Fondelle, "Everyman's dream woman, entangled hopelessly in a capitalist web of sexual fantasy in which half formed images and elusive innuendoes tease and titilate as Fiona displays something that is, in fact, unobtainable. Purchaser and provider are equally degraded." Again *The Jewish Echo*.

Angie Rew directed this sequel to *The Complete History of Rock 'n' Roll*, with great flair and there were contributions to the script from most of the Company. This was a new departure for Wildcat, and one of our more successful attempts at collective writing.

David Hicks and Terry Neason
in *Confessin' the Blues*
Photo Antonia Reeve

JOY IS IN THE CHILD

Father
You have given me
Life

Joy is in the child
In her infancy
Wisdom in the child
Perfect harmony
Mystics seek the child
In their memory
God in Heaven
What the hell is goin' on?

Father
You have given me
Life eternally
Let us walk with thee
Praise the holy He
He who let us be

Each little flower that opens
Each little bird that sings
He made their glowing colours
He made their tiny wings

God in Heaven
Father of Creation

Your Father,
Who works in Govan
It was him that gave you your name
He works for us
His word is law in this house as his father's
Was in his house
It's him that gives us our weekly wage
And he doesn't get into debt
And he doesn't have debtors
And he believes in eternal damnation
And he believes in God and the Devil
And he brings home the bacon
And the power
And the glory
For being your father
A man

In the beginning
There was nothing
Absolutely nothing
Not a blessed thing
I mean literally
Hee-haw
Except the Heavenly Father, that is
And God so loved the world
he sent forth a serpent
on the third page
And so sin was created
Dearly Beloved, do you fear the Lord?

Scared to death.

Brethren all humankind is born in sin saving the Lord Jesus
the Heavenly Father's only son born of a virgin so there was
no hanky-panky involved so saith the Heavenly Father's
Book and that's the gospel truth.

God in Heaven

Father

Father

Father
You have given me
Guilt

Joy is in the child
In her infancy
Knowledge in the child
when she starts to be
What we teach the child
That's what she will see

Careful what you do
Careful what you say
Watch your poetry
Doesn't run away
With the facts of life
Watch the child at play

See that frown
Wrinkle her forehead
Have you seen it before?
What have you done?
Hang around
Watch how she moves where
Have you seen that before?
Are you the one?

We are in the child
We are in her eyes
When we teach the child
Do we realise
What we steal away
If we tell her lies?

God in Heaven
Even Mother Nature
Has to be a Father

Father
You have given me
Guilt and puberty
Moral agony
Holy Moses
What the hell is goin' on?

BAMBINO MIO

Bambino
Bambino Mio
Wee Bambino
Bambino Mine

What a strange and magic mystery it seems to be
How you came into the world from deep inside of me
Seems to me you are the finest child I'll ever see
Who's your mammy and your daddy, hen?

Bambino
Bambino Mio
Wee Bambino
Bambino Mine

How you grew inside my body from the very first
Till it seemed I'd have to have you or I'd have to burst
Now you've got to be the centre of the Universe
Who's your mammy and your daddy, hen?

Bambino
Bambino Mio
Wee Bambino
Bambino Mine

Will your mammy and your daddy change your nappy, hen,
When you wake up in the middle of the night?
Will your daddy take his turn or is it mammy once again?
That's right!
Ah — ah — ah

Bambino
Bambino Mio
Wee Bambino
Bambino mine

David McNiven
in Confessin' the Blues

Photo Antonia Reeve

HEAVIES' RIFF

Wouldn't it be nice to cry
Unashamed of the tears in your eye
To be gentle and coy and shy
To have fun without alibi?

What a drag to be butch all day long
To look tough and sing mean macho songs
Buggin' phones breakin' bones — what a bore
To chew gum and spit on the floor . . .

But life has a singular plan
In the role of masculine man
In wolf's clothes we can't be meek as sheep
Oh, to be able to weep . . .

Wouldn't it be nice once or twice
To be sweet as ice sugar mice
To kiss babies play ludo and dice
Wouldn't it be nice to be nice?

THE QUEEN OF MY DREAMS

The queen of my dreams is dead,
The lover I've never known.
I gather they took her head
And put a new one on the throne.
The queen is dead —
Long live the queen
In the pages of a magazine.

The queen of my dreams is born
She looks a lot like the first
She really gives me the horn
Feel as if I'm going to burst
The promises
Of joyous lust
You hold them and they turn to dust.

Why can't I be satisfied?
Why can't I be satisfied?

The images on the gloss
I see them but I can't touch.
Why do I get a sense of loss?
The offer seems to be so much!
The queen is dead
In black and white.
Looks like another lonely night.

She seems to be flesh and blood.
She seems to be really real.
She says she'll burst into bud
As soon as I reach and feel
The queen is dead
The pages lie
The queen is dead and so am I.

Why can't I be satisfied?
Why can't I be satisfied?

1982 or ANY MINUTE NOW

This show toured for over a year and marked a popular breakthrough for the Company. An enormous range of venues included Stornoway, Kirkwall and Wick, the Citizens' in Glasgow and the Royal Lyceum in Edinburgh, London, Dublin and Stockholm, and the dozens of community centres around Scotland which now made up our regular touring circuit.

It was also a breakthrough in other ways. There was very little spoken dialogue — almost the whole being sung. This was now possible only because we had a group of considerable musical maturity and, in Terry Neason, a singer capable of handling a part of truly operatic proportions.

The show struck a raw nerve in Scotland, the United States No 1 aircraft carrier off the coast of Europe, and was embraced by the Peace Movement as a campaigning weapon at a time when the fear of those other weapons was uniting an enormous number of people in the struggle against the accelerating arms race.

David Anderson and Billy Johnstone
in *1982 or Any Minute Now*
Photo George Oliver

Hilton MaCrae
in *1982 or Any Minute Now*
Photo David Corio

I AM BECOME DEATH

MARY
Where the street used to be
there's nothing nothing
where the house used to be
there's nothing nothing
where on earth on earth am I

Where the school used to be
the grass is growing
where the shop used to be
the wind is blowing
where on earth on earth am I

CHORUS
In the sky the sun
turning black as ash
In the sky the moon
turning red as blood
Hide your eyes there is
white fire in the sky
Mary's in confusion
nightmare and delusion
everything is changing
moving rearranging
Mourners at a wedding
christening the coffin
burying the baby
dancing round the widow
Slaughterhouse for rental
suitable for couple
hospital conversion
burials cremation
Kindergarten offer
ready for the oven
Hiroshima Travel
holiday for Mary
Every time that Mary turns
she sees another lie

MARY
You have stood at the abyss
you have stared into hell
you have seen the children burning
and you have not drawn back

CHORUS
I am become death
the destroyer of worlds

SING THOSE HYMNS

MARY
Sing those hymns in unison
Memorise the word
Onward christian soldiers
Marching for the Lord
Teach the little children
Everything you may
Lord our God's a jealous god
On the Judgement Day

CHORUS
So bring on the apocalypse
And the pestilence
And the fire
To purify all god's sinners
Is that the sound of distant drumming?
Lord, we know we've got it coming
Send down a judgement
On all God's children

HEADMASTER
Come all ye sinners
And listen to my speech
The kingdom of heaven
Is out of mortal reach
Except for the humble
Who learn to obey
The Lord gonna get you
On the judgement day
Hellfire and damnation
Will be yours as sure as fate
Ain't no good for the sinner to speculate
Ain't that great!

HEADMASTER AND CHORUS
Did you hear about Noah, children?
    Noah, children?
The Lord came down
    The Lord came down
Said everybody's been so bad
Gonna send you all a flood
So build an ark 'cos everybody's gonna drown

Did you hear about Jericho?
　Jericho?
The walls fell down
　The walls fell down
And everybody got to know
The power of God when the trumpets blow
With one quick blast he devastated that old town

Did you hear what the Lord did?
　The Lord did?
To Sodom and Gomorrah?
　Sodom and Gomorrah?
The fire was all the sinners' fault
Lot's wife deserved to turn to salt
He can do it once He can do it again tomorrow

'Cos they were people like you and me
　Sinners!
And we'll share their destiny
　Sinners!
And that's the lesson of history
　Sinners!

A fiery flood
A burning lake
To cleanse us all
For Jesus sake

CHORUS
So bring on the apocalypse
And the pestilence
And the fire
To purify all God's sinners
Is that the sound of distant drumming?
Lord, we know we've got it coming
Send down a judgement
On all God's children

MARY
I will burn in the fire
Doesn't matter what I do
And the sins of my father
Will be visited on me

God above
Loves the little children
As they kneel and pray
I believe
Jesus will protect me
Till the judgement day
The God of love
Saves us from our suff'ring
When He sweeps away
All God's children
Children

Terry Neason and Doreen Cameron
in *1982 or Any Minute Now*
Photo David Corio

HEADMASTER
The first lesson is history
Starting in a thousand years B.C.
The Grecian Army engineered a trap
And wiped the Trojans right off the map
Doesn't say what might have happened
To the children

The Greeks beat the Trojans
And the Romans beat the Greeks
And the Muslims beat the Hindus
And the Christians beat the Sikhs
The Kings beat the Princes
And the Yankees beat the Geeks
The Whiteys beat the Niggers
And the Normals beat the Freaks
The sharks eat the minnows
And the mighty beat the weak
And the cannon beats the dagger
And the forthright beat the meek
The history books do not speak
About the children
Children

MARY
That's the lesson of history
Talkin' about hegemony
Kings and Princes of the mighty nations
Negotiating with devastation
You don't get a lot of information
About the children
Children

CHORUS
So bring on the armaments
And the combatants
And the fire
To satisfy all ambition
Is that the sound of battle raging
Once again the war is waging
Another sacrifice
For all our children
Children
Children

WILL ON YOU

Never mind my cheeky little uni-sex ass
Never mind the chicken-shit you read in the press
I ain't no transexual
Ain't no hermaphrodite
Gonna show you my manhood
And that'll serve you right
I'm gonna give you
The big one
I'm gonna impose
My will on you
I'm gonna whip out
The big gun
You'll get a big dose
Of will on you
Will on you will on you

Don'tcha think its sexy when I threaten to come
Over your submission 'cos you're under my thumb
Isn't that erotic
I'll pin you to the floor
Make you so neurotic
Till you yell for more
I'm gonna give you
The big one

Ain't so much my muscle
As my attitude
Hit you with my missile
To your gratitude

Better just surrender to my obvious charms
Subordinate your gender in my muscular arms
Good-morning little schoolgirl
I'm a man (M-A-N)
The men don't know
But the little girls understand
I'm gonna give you
The big one
I'm gonna impose
My will on you
I'm gonna whip out
The big gun
You'll get a big dose
Of will on you
Will on you will on you

MARY'S DREAM

Didn't they used to slay
the bringer of bad news
in the hope that the truth
might disappear?
Didn't they used to slay
the messenger who came
with the word of war
that the king had feared?

CHORUS
Prophets shall be without
all honour in their land.
How could she know what we
have never seen?
Know her face
knew her father
he was the funny one
and the funny one she's always been

MARY
Through this nightmare
I have wondered
where I saw you all before
tried to recognise your faces
tried to see behind the door

Now I've stumbled on the answer
none of you are who you seem
I have met you in a nightmare
in a mad recurring dream

Met the Judge and Prosecution
met the Man who makes munitions
General and Civil Servant
Clerk of Court, Psychiatrist
Counsel for Defence and Usher
in a mad recurring dream

None of you
recognise me
I was the witness
I'm the one
I'm the lonely passer-by

Terry Neason
in *1982 or Any Minute Now*   Photo David Corio

I was there
I was watching
I was the only one
The only one who didn't die

CHORUS
The wind blows over the broken bricks
of a silent city at dawn
and cuts the cheek
like broken glass
and the woman passes on
by gutted shells and skeletons
of factories and tenements
and remnants of communities
and the woman passes on

MARY
In my dream
I see you all
driving by
in limousines
no despairing
only staring
out of tinted window screens
you have scuttled
from your burrows
in the bowels of the earth
it spewed you forth
in my dream

In my dream
I see you all
pointing out
as if you knew
no surmises
no surprises
nothing shocking in the view
making for the
City Chambers
in the ruins of the town
they set you down
in my dream

None of you
recognise me
I was the witness
I'm the one
I'm the lonely passer-by
I was there
I was watching
I was the only one
The only one who didn't die
in my dream

In my dream
I see you all
passing thro'
the marble halls
those invited
are excited
laughter echoes off the walls
gathering for
celebration
for a banquet for the few
the few who knew
in my dream

These are the men
that we never see
who plan to steal
our lives away
they hide away
from you and me
and hatch their plans
in secrecy

H.M.V.

1982 was also a breakthrough because it allowed us to put together a brand new Wildcat Company to tour H.M.V. while the old guard were abroad. A number of talented young performers who were soon to become Wildcat regulars joined the group; Elaine C. Smith, Myra McFadyen, Lesley Robertson. John McGlynn, who had been in the original 7:84 production of the show, returned to the cast.

H.M.V. was a punk's eye-view of the music biz, and our punk was Tam Skelly, and his band were The Snotters. This show about the mass media has proved immensely popular with young audiences and since our production it has been put on at the Half Moon in London, and in Perth, Western Australia — which would indicate that the machinations of the multi-national record companies are as clearly understood there as they are here.

The Company
in *HMV*
Photo Sean Hudson

Myra McFadyen and Billy Elliot
in *HMV*
Photo David Williams

BRAND NEW

Bull shit What you taught me at
School shit All that
Rule shit Where to go what to do but the
Punk folk The ones you treated like
Junk folk All the stoned and the
Drunk folk

We don't have much but at least we got
Music For the people not the
Chosen few.
Punk music makes the dead kids feel
Brand New

Don't you think it's time that you
Told us Told us the truth and not the
Same old spew?
Here we are and we wanna hear something
Brand New.

They tell ya they don't
Need ya! But they'll clothe and they'll
Feed ya! Feed ya crap from the
Media!
As you stand in the queue for your
Hand out But be sure you don't
Stand out Don't you put no
Demand out.

I'm the man that's expressin' the
Feelin' Makes me feel that it's
All I can do.
Punk music makes the dead kids feel
Brand New.

We are the crowd
We're the eternal crowd
We can always be depended on to be the crowd
We are alone
Individually
But together we have a voice that's good and loud
We get to feel
Brand New
We are the crowd
We're the forgotten crowd

But we'll never let you forget that we're the crowd
Me on my own
You don't look at me
But together we'll make you see that we're the crowd
We get to feel
Brand New

Dead kids All the ones with no
Bread kids The ones you knocked on the
Head kids The one's you kicked on
The buroo We don't have to
Spell out That we don't wanna
Shell out Just to pay for a
Sell out
Are you dumb can't you feel the
Frustration? Which is why we wanna
Frustrate You
We'll listen if you're gonna say something
Brand New.

Myra McFadyen and Elaine C Smith   Photo David Williams
in *HMV*

E A D A E

E A D A E
It's as simple as 1 2 3
E A D A E
It's no secret mystery
Just do it
Do it
Do it yourself

E A D A E
You don't need no music degree
E A D A E
Don't you bother with doh ray me
Just do it
Do it
Do it yourself

That's the secret of rock 'n' roll
You don't have to be no Nat King Cole
It's the music for you the music for me
3 chords and you're on your way
Let no-one tell you that you can't play
When you boogie what a buzz when you change the key

Maybe it's no symphony
With a load of fancy harmony
But it makes you feel good for a little while
You don't need to pay no tutor's fee
Just to strum a simple melody
Sing do it
Do it
Do it yourself

You don't need a bunch of superstars
Playin' clichés on their new guitars
Gettin' richer with a heap of hackneyed words
You don't need a load of fashion clothes
Just to know what Peter Frampton knows
All you have to do is learn some simple chords

E A D A E
You don't need no music degree
E A D A E
Don't you bother with doh ray me
Just do it
Do it
Do it
Do it yourself

MA HERO

Sometimes
Only sometimes
But never for long
I could cry like a baby
For no reason at all
Rememb'ring
Just rememb'ring
When he was young
When he seemed to me to be ten feet tall

Now look at my hero
He could have been something
He could have been a man among many
He could have been a man among men
It used to be the world was his oyster
Now it's just a cage
Now it's just a pen
Look at my hero
He's useless he's nothing
I hate him for bein' a loser
I wish I was sixteen again

Sometimes
Only sometimes
But never for long
He looks just for a moment
Like the man he used to be
Good times
We had good times
When we were young
When he was the man who would set me free

Now look at my hero
He's got no ambition
He used to have a fire in his body
He used to be my champion then
Now he's just an old lazy dreamer
Sittin' in a chair
Only half a man
Look at my hero
A pale imitation
I hate him for bein' a loser
I wish I was sixteen again

YOUNG AMERICAN

I'm a young American an' I don't
Trust the President
Got muh guitar in muh hand
Gonna overthrow the government
I believe the tide will turn
I put my faith in the nation's youth
Because the death-dealing
Con-cealing
Oil-stealing
Administration
Gives me the feeling
They ain't never gonna tell the truth

I'm a young American an' I'm singing
In Greenwich Village
Gonna tell ma fellow man 'bout America's
Rape and pillage
I believe the time will come
People will stand together as one
And the Imperialist
Capitalist
Evangelist
Old man Uncle Sam
Repressed Calvinist
Will no longer rule by the gun

I'm a young American an' I'm signed to a
Record company
Gonna make some records about the
Nation's foreign policy
Gonna get some changes made
By the word of rock 'n' roll
An' I'm gonna resist
The revisionist
Feminist
Radical chic
Women that persist
In tryin' to get inside mah soul

I'm a young American an' I'm
Into psychedelia
Hopin' you can understand
What I'm tryin' to tell ya
All you kids are foolishly
Makin' a hero out of Bob
Just a poem-yellin'
Best-sellin'
Bad-spellin'
Dude don't you see
What I'm tellin'
You it's the people's job

I'm a young American gettin'
Older by the minute
Gettin' cynical 'bout the western world
And everything that's in it
The people have let me down real bad
Gonna turn my back on you
I got my own crazy
Kinda hazy
Kamikaze
Personal problems
I'm depressed and lazy
Whatcha expect me to do?

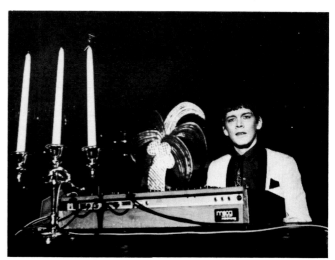

Rab Handleigh
in *A Bunch of Fives*

Photo Sean Hudson

Mike Travis, Kenny Potter, Rab Handleigh, Terry Neason and David
Anderson in *A Bunch of Fives*
Photo Sean Hudson

A BUNCH OF FIVES

In the Spring of 1983 we had our first stab at more or less
straight cabaret. Regular writers, Anderson and
MacLennan were joined by Liz Lochhead, Sean Hardie and
Tom Leonard, and were heartened to find that they shared
with them Wildcat's recurring obsession with the media. *A
Bunch of Fives* took T.V. as both its medium and its
principal target — partly in revenge. At a previous
production a young member of the audience had piped up in
a shrill and penetrating voice, "Mum, I'm bored. Can't we
change the channel?"

Despite the competition from television and the bleak
financial climate, Wildcat had now established a broad
popular audience.

The collaboration with Liz, Sean and Tom was to prove
fruitful for the future. Tom was to write more material for
It's a Free Country and *Wildnights at the Tron*. Liz gave us
Same Difference in the following year, and Sean directed
Bless My Soul for Channel Four.

YOU'VE GOT TO LAUGH

When the boss has bought a Bentley
and you've had to sell your Daf
        you've got to laugh
When he's dining in the Bistro
and you're choking in the caff
        you've got to laugh
When his earnings rise like pastry
yours are sinking like a graph
        you've got to laugh
When you haven't got an earthly
of living like the other half
        you've got to laugh
Every time you pass his mansion
and compare it to your gaff
        you've got to laugh
While he's swilling Chateau Margaux
and there's plonk in your carafe
        you've got to laugh
When you see his mohair jacket
and your corduroy is naff
        you've got to laugh
When he smokes he smokes Havana
you smoke rollies full of chaff
        you've got to laugh
He's got a sauna and jacuzzi
you've a ring around the baff
        you've got to laugh
He's got a valet, maid and butler
and your wife is on his staff
        you've got to laugh
Talk of brassneck his is one that
would embarrass a giraffe
        you've got to laugh
Sod you sucker I'm alright Jack
ought to be his epitaph
        you've got to laugh

INTENSIVE CARE

The light is out it's steely blue
And in the electronic hue
A figure in an easy chair
Is drifting in Intensive Care
A tube provides his every need
A constant pre-digested feed
A blend of easy soothing pap
And subtle lies and poisoned crap

In Intensive Care In Intensive Care

The Patient spent an easy night
Responding well to sound and sight
The patient's appetite is fair
The patient's in Intensive Care
The patient's state is comfortable
He musn't get excitable
The medication's working well
He must be left to rest a spell

In Intensive Care In Intensive Care

Analgesic Anaesthetic Disinfectant Vaccination
Anti-toxin Preparation Tourniquet and Embrocation
Sanitise and Cauterise and Sterilise the Nation
And cut off the flow

He's suffering a loss of will
The patient is susceptible
To what the night nurse has to say
The patient's mind has slipped away

In Intensive Care In Intensive Care

In television's great debate
The experts can participate
The television viewer's role
is listening to what he's told
In television fairyland
the programme planners have it planned
To cut off the flow

In television wonderland,
The laughter and applause is canned
The television audience
can witness the experience
The television fantasy
of living in democracy

In Intensive Care In Intensive Care

If it's TV status quo
You might as well be dead
If it's living then it's
Turn the world on its head

WELCOME TO PARADISE

While we were putting this little extravaganza together, Feri Lean, who had been a founder member of the group and our first Administrator, was working feverishly to get the first Glasgow Mayfest off the ground. We premièred *Welcome to Paradise* at the Festival in the Mitchell Theatre. Neither Wildcat nor Mayfest would enjoy the popular support they do had it not been for Feri's tireless work.

The MacLeods are victims of the Highland Clearances. Some of the family move to the slums of Glasgow, some to the sunnier climes of California. Their descendants lose touch, but in 1983 Sheena MacLeod in Glasgow wins a competition in *The Daily Record* to meet her idol — Californian rock star, Jane Armadillo. When they meet, these two very different women discover they are distant cousins . . .

Scotland's relationship with the U.S. has been a constant source of joy and depression for us, and it provides a most insistent itch which we have returned to scratch from time to time. Some people find it peculiar that we should lambast Imperialist Uncle Sam in songs which owe as much to the Mississippi Delta as they do to the Clyde Valley — perhaps Tam's Song in *Heather up your Kilt* goes some way to explaining the paradox.

Terry Neason
in *Welcome to Paradise*
Photo David Williams

THE HOUSE IS DAMP

OVERTURE
Once upon a time
In a black house
On a grey island
Lived a family
The women were weavers
They waulked the tweed
The men were fishers
And they sailed the sea

And we sail the stormy ocean
On a boat too small for comfort
On a wind intent on murder
For the fishin'
As we sail the cruel ocean
Like our fathers did before us
We sing as did our fathers
Songs of wishin'

And Tir-na-nog is just beyond the sea
Out of reach
Of the livin'
There once were giants
Who strode across the sea
To a beach
We call Heaven
Tir-na-nog is paradise on the horizon
For the giants
Where they stay
Forever young

But mortal men must fish the ocean
In a boat as did our fathers
And if we drown our sons will follow
For the fishin'
And as we brave the bloody ocean
Women wait by the harbour
And they sing as did their mothers
Songs of waitin'

Ochone, ochone, ochone, ochone,
ochone, ochone, ochone, ochone,
Women sing ochone, ochone

Fishers fish in fear of weather
Sailors sing and sailors blether
Women work and pull together
Oh sisters waulk the tweed
Women work and pull together
Oh sisters waulk the tweed

Sailors sing of lands of plenty
Giant steps and giant deeds
Women work in the land of reality
Oh sisters waulk the tweed
Women work in the land of reality
Oh sisters waulk the tweed

Pass the tweed and stretch the tweed
Pull the tweed and pound the tweed
Pass the tweed and work the tweed
Waulk the tweed till your fingers bleed
Women work in the land of reality
Oh sisters waulk the tweed

Myra McFadyen, Elaine C Smith and Terry Neason
in *Welcome to Paradise*
Photo David Williams

Sailors sail the sulky sea
Women work the withered land
Sailors sing of eternity
Women sing to the job in hand
Sailors sing of eternity
Women sing to the job in hand

Fishers fish the bloody sea
Women weave and bear the seed
Heaven's not for you and me
Oh sisters waulk the tweed
Heaven's not for you and me
Oh sisters waulk the tweed

They say that heaven
Is just beyond the sea
Out of reach of the livin'
And only giants can spend eternity
On the beach
They call heaven

Paradise is on the horizon
Why can't heaven
Be right here?
Why can't heaven
Be right here?

This house is damp
This house is clammy
This house is gonnae kill your mammy
This house is not fit for people to live in
The walls are wet
Your blankets soakin'
Your daddy's old before his time:
My darlin's chokin'
This house is surely a long way from heaven

As in the Holy Roman Empire
Remembered fondly by the landlord
We serve the God of Power
So in the mighty British Empire
Money talks and money needs your land
Money needs the landlord's land

The house is burning
Our land is taken
The hill we planted
Will turn to bracken
The people cleared in the name of the Empire

The God has spoken
No trace of pity
The family broken
Some to the city
Some cross the sea in the name of the Empire

GLASGOW SONG

What have they got in common the common working men
The women and the children who left the burning glen
Who traded burning cottages for furnace forge and smoke
Cleared from their highland countryside the
                                    common working folk?

    Raw materials

What have they got in common
                              what common future planned
The fisher and the weaver who left the rotting land
Who left behind the famine to starve in single ends
And feed the needs of industry and die in single ends?

    Raw materials

Through the fields of summer barley
                              golden fields of oats and wheat
Grazing cattle pause to listen to the sound of trudging feet
Land of gates and walls and fences
                              country mansions so discreet
Hidden from the eyes of strangers
                              and the sound of trudging feet

Over fields of hidden treasures seams of coal and iron ore
Innocent and unsuspecting what the future holds in store
Watching hidden at a window calculating calm and cold
Stands a man with dreams of labour
                              turning coal and iron to gold

A man with a feel for the power of machinery
Can build a dream he sees in his mind
He can gather together the raw materials
And shape the world to his own design

He sees bridges that leap over river and estuary
Engines that roar he sees in his dream
They span mountain and moorland cross every barrier
The sound of progress the sound of steam

Liners that reach every ocean and continent
Cargoes of wealth from lands overseas
He can gather together into his factories
He will be master of, he will be master of,
He will be master of all

    Raw materials raw materials

Through the freezing winter evenings
                  death is stalking through the streets
Casting shadows on the buildings
                  bringing fear to all he meets
City of tuberculosis scarlet fever whooping cough
Typhoid stillbirth malnutrition starving hunger carries off

    Raw materials

Fire the coal and fell the timber
                  melt the ore and forge the steel
Turn the engines sweat and labour
                  swing the crane and lay the keel
Drive the rivet drive the labour labour rivet plate to plate
Launch the liner on the river labour makes the Empire great

Build the workshop of the Empire
                  tunnel hammer pump and mill
Pressing turning weaving mining
                  labour power and labour skill
Build the fortunes of the Empire
                  labour muscle sweat and toil
Empire built on sweated labour iron coal and steel and oil

No time to think of the victims or casualties
No time to stop or to hesitate
He must drive on relentless fashion his fantasies
He must be master of his own fate

Nothing must stand between him and his destiny
Nothing deter him or bar his way
He's the man of the future the maker of history
He must be master of, he must be master of,
He must be master of all

YERBA BUENA

And so we sailed the bloody ocean
To a place called Nova Scotia
Which we found dark and forbidding
Like the island

But California is just across the plain
Gold and peaches lush and givin'
Under the prairie sky we drove the wagon train
To a beach close to heaven

And California is far across the sea
Golden peaches lush and givin'
Under the prairie sky they drove the wagon train
To a beach close to heaven

We used to call thees bay Yerba Buena
Was here I used to have my hacienda
Don Cortez stole thee coastland from thee injun
And try to save their soul with his religion
From Tijuana
To San Mateo
The mission bells ring Buenos Dias
Thees land belongs to God and the Chicano

One day as I was having my siesta
My head she hurt from brandy at fiesta
I'm wakened by my son (hees name ees Ringo)
He says thees bay ees full of bloody gringos
Eet was thee gold rush
And they were miners
The year was eighteen forty nine
I theenk that's why we called them forty-niners

Adios Yerba Buena
Buenas noches, Mexico
Hasta la vista, etcetera
Hello San Francisco

They came from far and wide and Pennsylvania
Their eyes were crazy weeth thee monomania
I theenk some of them come from Transylvania
From Caledonia via Nova Scotia
From Tijuana
To Sacramento
Thee mission bells reeng un lamento
Thee land we stole ees stolen by thee Gringo

Adios Yerba Buena
Buenas noches Mexico
Hasta la vista, etcetera
Hello San Francisco

Tir-na-nog is paradise on the horizon
For the giants
Where we'll stay
Forever young
Where we'll stay
Forever young

THE RENT STRIKE SONG

The family came to Glasgow
It was eighteen forty nine
And the men worked in the ship-yard and the mine
The work was here in Glasgow
But the wages soon were spent
To feed and clothe the weans and for the rent
The McLeods from the cold grey island
From the black house tae the slum
And we wished tae God we didnae have to come
The family came to Glasgow
And we've been here to this day
And now they've taken your daddy and sent him far away
To war
This house is damp
This house is clammy
This house is gonnae
Kill your mammy
This house is not fit for people to live in

And while your daddy's fightin'
There are some who're makin' guns
To help the British Empire beat the Huns
The workin' folk of Glasgow
In these shitey tenements
Are told the Factor's gonnae raise the rent
Weirs the munitions factory
Make profits from the war
And some are makin' money
The factor thinks he'll ask for more
The women folk of Glasgow
Have been beatin' on a drum
And refusin' to go penniless for a slum
We told the Factor:
This house is damp
This house is clammy
And you're no gettin'
Another penny
This house is not fit for people to live in
We banged drums
We rang bells
We blew our trumpets
We shouted slogans
We told the Factor to raffle his doughnut
And we won
A wee victory
It can be done

AND IT WAS DAMP

We told the factor
But youse are well aware
Of the story so far in the Gorbals
The McLeods who came to the Gorbals
Have been fightin' ever since

We fought the Landlord
We fought the Redcoats
We fought the Empire
And the McDonalds
And if we hadnae been fightin' each other
We might have won

I fought the Factor
The bloody miser
You think that's bloody
I fought the Kaiser
Well you should never have gone in the first place

We fought the Bosses
In the recession
I fought the Proddies
In the depression
And if we hadnae been fightin' each other . . .

I fought wi' Franco
I fought the Factor
I fought the Nazis
I fought the Factor
I fought the Baltic, the Fleet and the Cumbie

We fought for wages
We fought for rations
We fought for ages
And generations
We fought for Celtic
We fought for Rangers
And Partick Thistle

Partick Thistle?

Myra McFadyen and Elaine C Smith
in *Welcome to Paradise*
Photo David Williams

For UCS and occupations
And tribulations
And if we hadnae been fightin' each other . . .

I fought in Aden
I fought in Kenya
I fought in Cyprus
And Malaya
We fought the Tories
We fought wi' Wilson
And Partick Thistle
Got promotion
I fought the Factor
About conditions
I fought the Glasgow
Corporation
We fought to get a new house from the Council
And we won

In nineteen sixty nine
We got a brand new flat
In Hutchesontown
Mediterranean-style
And it wis damp
And it wis clammy
We got together
Kicked up a rammy
We went on rent-strike
We signed petitions
Had delegations
And demonstrations
We fought to get a new house from the Council
And we won
A wee victory
It can be done

They closed the whole scheme down
We got a brand new house
In Toryglen
White-painted terraces

And it was damp

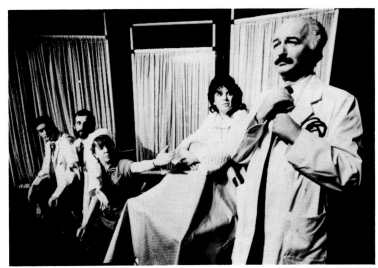

The Company   Photo Sean Hudson
in *Bed Pan Alley*

BED PAN ALLEY

The Conservative Government decided the way to cure the ills of the Health Service was to appoint managers and to run it like a supermarket. A healthy turnover of beds concentrating on lines that shifted quickly. "This week's special offer — Varicose Veins. Of course, if you are a geriatric or suffer from some chronic disorder we can't waste precious shelf space on the likes of you".

Here are extracts of some reviews written by the pupils of Camelon High School: "Wildcat are very good actors. They do different styles. I like them. I would go again because it is very good and you have a laugh watching them if they make a mistake."
"The show was great and it was much better than what I had expected. The singing was good and it was very funny too, unlike any other plays."
"The music is good. I got carried away."

Those who make their living reviewing were less able to agree with us or with each other.
"Bed Pan Alley is a lazy and superficial piece of work."
Joyce MacMillan, *The Guardian*.
"I have no reservations whatsoever, they are back on form. A brilliant start to 1984". Mary Brennan, *Glasgow Herald*.

BEWARE THE POET

Beware the Poet who comes to you
Singing out songs of love and romance
Maybe you don't know it but his heart's not true
He's looking out for the number one chance
He sings so sweetly
You give your heart completely
And you comply so neatly
With his plans

Beware the Poet who sounds so nice
Sounds as if he's your friend
Maybe he won't show it but he's solid ice
He's empty no matter what he pretends
The drum machine keeps perfect time
Makes the singer sound sublime
But it all comes down to rhyme
In the end

Beware the Poet
And his silver tongue
And the empty words
In the song he's sung
Beware the Poet

GIMME TRUTH

Got this feeling
I can't deny
My head is reeling
Full of lies
Small voice is crying
Sighs as it cries
Please stop the lying
Please stop the lies

Gimme truth
Nothing less than truth
I don't want your word in advance
Gimme truth
Nothing but the truth
It's more beautiful than romance
Don't give me rhetoric
Don't give me promises
Don't give me guarantees please
Don't give me bullshit
Gimme truth.

AGITPROP

She asked me if I'd be at her
Cheese and wine soirée
Said "What's the role of theatre
In the present day?
Should it be metaphysical
Or better still allegorical
At times a little whimsical
Or should it be historical?"

Went to a convention
Of performing arts
Asked me "Could I mention
How I approach my parts
Should theatre be rhetorical
Theological or empirical
Paradoxical, metaphorical
Or is one just a vehicle?"

I had to say I'm into
Agitation
Propaganda
Information
Gimme candour
Direct Action
Disobedience
Satisfaction
Inconvenience
Agitprop
Over the top
Political bop
Don't ever stop
Till they drop

What's your view on realism?
What's your theory?
Stylisation, naturalism?
To be or not to be?
To be quite meritorious
Should a play be mysterious?
Isn't art awfully serious?
You're making me delirious!

I had to say I'm into
Agitation
Propaganda
Information
Gimme candour
Direct Action
Disobedience
Satisfaction
Inconvenience
Agitprop
Over the top
Political bop
Don't ever stop
Till they drop.

David Anderson
in *Bed Pan Alley*
Photo Sean Hudson

DEAD LIBERTY

We wrote this piece at the prompting of our friend and comrade, Tam Mylchreest, Pit Delegate at Castle Hill Colliery, and later to become one of the miners who were victimised by the N.C.B. During it's Autumn tour in 1984, we were to see at first hand the great sacrifices the mining communities were making in their epic struggle for the whole of the working class. Their defeat left no doubt that the Tories were determined to break the power of organised labour and exact revenge for their losses in 1972 and 1974.

In our researching we were given unstinting help by the members of the Stirling Miners Women's Support Group, and a lot of the humour in the tale, and much else besides, came from their lives. One of the great pleasures of working for Wildcat is in making so many new friends with each new project.

One of the highlights of the tour was a performance given at the community centre in Bowhill — the home of the Bowhill Players and the 'Miner' playwright, Joe Corrie. *The* highlight had to be the night at Stirling Miners' Welfare Club, where over three hundred men and women from the coalfield cheered us on like a football team in a home derby, and finished the evening, after a very moving presentation of miners' lamps to all the Company, with several choruses of "Here we go, Here we go, Here we go!"

MOTORWAY SONG

What's the point in education?
In a year or two
You'll know all you need to know,
You'll know a Mr you-know-who
They'll know you know, you're you-know-what
He'll know what he must do
Something old, something new,
Something borrowed, something blue . . .

Cars going past on the motorway,
People with somewhere to go.
Traffic is fast on the motorway
By my window.

You'll know all you need to know
Within a year or three.
What you know is what you get
And what you get is what you see
One at school and one at home
And one at nursery
And another little brother in January . . .

Cars going past on the motorway,
People with somewhere to go.
Traffic is fast on the motorway
By my window.
And the world turns, leaving me behind.

When you know the facts of life
You know the facts don't lie.
In fact, the fact of life is that
Your life's a fact until you die.
What would you do, suppose you knew
The wherefore or the why
Of the stars, life on Mars,
Or the cars going by?

Cars going past on the motorway,
People with somewhere to go.
Traffic is fast on the motorway
By my window.

Just down the motorway
There's a pit
It's not far to go.
As I pass by on the motorway
You can wave from the window,
And the coal burns,
Makes the world turn,
There's no sunshine
Down the mine.

WHAT NEXT?

I told the boys when they were young
Don't do what your daddy done
It's dirty work and it's badly paid
Get yourself some other trade
You never know from day to day
When you'll have to move away
Leave your home and all you know
That's if there's somewhere to go

What next?
Do we go or do we stay?
What next?
Some one knows but they won't say

I used to say I didn't like
When your daddy went on strike
I'm feeding weans and he's in the way
Instead of bringing home his pay
But then at last the penny dropped
That nothing happened till he stopped
Now this is what I tell the boys
Be like your dad you have no choice

What next?
'Cos you never know the day
What next?
Some one knows but they won't say

Is he going to move again?
Don't know where don't know when
When will he be home for tea?
Half past five half past three?
Everything is getting dear
Will there be a strike this year?
Win or lose it's all one
Still you're back where you begun

What next?
Do we quit or do we stay?
What next?
God knows it's time
We got our way

DEAD LIBERTY

When they take your work
Treat you like a jerk
And mock your poverty
Someone taps your phone
This is what is known
As Dead Liberty

When the hoods and crooks
Get to cook the books
And rob you endlessly
And the judge is bribed
This is best described
As Dead Liberty

And when your friendly neighbourhood cop
Seems to go right over the top
And to see his brief
Not to catch a thief
But to stop you complainin'
By beatin' your brain in

When the guys with guns
Are the lucky ones
Who get to wander free
Then the populace
Recognise a case
Of Dead Liberty

And when your daily newspaper tries
To pull the wool right over your eyes
And disseminate
Prejudice and hate
And the lies they're expressing
And the truth they're suppressing

When the cops protect
Those you most suspect
Of daylight robbery
Then it's time to say
That there ain't no way
You can do this thing to me
We don't need no
Dead Liberty

Rab Handleigh   Photo Tom Hilton
in *Dead Liberty*

BUMS AND LOSERS

Care to join the
Bums and losers
Find some place to stay
In the garbage
In the shadow
Of the motorway

But for fortune
Goes the prayer
I could join the queue
Just a warning
Someone somewhere
Has big plans for you

In among the bald tyres and mattresses
Stroll around the barbed wire and plastic
Wander through the moonlight and roses
Find yourself a little space
And take your place
Amongst the trash

David Anderson and Steven Wren
in *Dead Liberty*
Photo Tom Hilton

THE CRACK

Everybody loves a winner
Hates a poor relation
Here's the offer
To the loser
By way of consolation

Come and join the worn-out appliances
Be another burned-out component
Rusting in the moonlight and roses
There's a battered old settee
For you and me
Amongst the trash

Do you wanna be that way?
Thanks but no thanks
In among the garbage
Just a little closure eh?
Thanks but no thanks
Think of the advantage

This invitation gives me no choice
This kind of freedom
Leaves me with no voice
Talk of controlling
The money supply
Supplies me with nothing
That's talk I don't buy
Thanks but no thanks.

Do I need the slag heap?
Am I really obsolete?
Care to join the flotsam
In among the jetsam?
Take your rightful place
Garbage of the human race?
Do you want to end your days
Underneath the motorways?
This invitation's no good to me
Participation in dead liberty —
Thanks but no thanks

The action in *The Crack* took place on an ingenious revolving set brought to you by our tireless and talented designer, Annette Gillies. Take a bow. While we are at it, will all the other choreographers, carpenters, technicians and other unseen and unsung heroes without whom
. . . take a bow.

The reason for the divided set was class, the British kind, upper and lower. On the one side, in Garthamlock, we give you the McGurks, on the other, in Knightsbridge, please welcome the Ponsonby-Havering-Strontiums.

Will the ladies take a bow from Sloane Square O.K. Yah? Orchid ffrench-ffrys — Elaine C. Smith; Fiona Ponsonby-Havering-Strontium Countess of Spittal — Elaine Collins; Antonia P.H.S., Dowager Countess of Spittal — Myra McFadyen. Now the gentlemen. Sir Charles ffrench-ffrys — David Hicks; Henry P.H.S., Viscount Dalwhinnie — Rab Handleigh; and finally Willie Ponsonby-Havering-Strontium, Earl of Spittal — David Anderson. And then there were those funny little people with their ghastly Glasgow accents, the McSomethingorothers.

A cracking tour ended with a run at the Citizens' in Glasgow that had something of the atmosphere of the old Alhambra *Five Past Eight* shows.

David Anderson and Myra McFadyen
in *The Crack*
Photo Anthony Brannan

THE CRACK

We didn't come to analyse.
We didn't come to theorise.
We didn't come to improvise, politicise,
Patronise you guys, or pull the wool over your eyes.
We didn't come to educate.
We didn't come to illustrate.
We didn't come to implicate the head of state,
Denigrate the interest rate, violate your garden gate.
We came for the crack.
We came for the crack.

We didn't come to bring you art.
We don't pretend to be that smart.
We don't bring you the party line.
We won't whine, drink your wine,
Or define the divine design.
We didn't come to bring culture to the masses.
We didn't come to polish your glasses.
We didn't pass our master class.
Stanislavsky, kiss my ass,
Stuff your motivation, Jack.
We came for the crack.
We came for the crack.

If you're only drinking watter
Then its hard to have a natter
But a session on the batter's
An entirely different matter.
With a whisky John the Baptist
Would be chatting on his platter.
Gie a sherry to your maiden aunt
She'll gie you all her patter.
Though the crack of John the Baptist
Would be better than the latter.
What's crack?
Crack's patter!

It's the flow of conversation
When you've had a small libation.
Call it vocal liberation.
Call it oral stimulation.
It's a mix of education
With a little syncopation.
It's a moving peroration.
Or it's gossip and sensation.
Crack's a calling, a vocation.
It's the pastime of the nation!
What's crack?
Crack's patter!

We didn't come to rock the boat.
We didn't come to win your vote.
We didn't come to get a quote, play the goat,
Make you change your coat
Or learn the words we say by rote.

The last time Wildcat hit the road
We made a Tory chap explode.
Michael Forsyth, a young MP,
Objected to Dead Liberty.
He didn't find the poster funny.
The whole thing wasted public money.
And Michael F. is bound to know
Although he never saw the show . . .

So no more miners,
No more shirkers,
No more lefties,
No more workers.
A Tory Party Cabaret
A Blue Revue, a right wing play,
An evening with the upper crust.
Don't miss it dahlings it's a must!

Elaine C Smith and David Anderson
in *The Crack*

Photo Anthony Brannan

KNIGHTSBRIDGE IS NICE

Knightsbridge is nice
Good class of neighbour
No-one has lice
And no-one votes Labour
Mayfair is mayhem
Kensington's crowded
And how about Hampstead?
It's practically Birmingham.

Barnes is a bore
Richmond is pretty
One can ignore
East of the city
Knightsbridge is splendid
Topping for shopping
Wapping sounds awful
Somewhere near Birmingham.

One has one's home in Hampshire
When the tourists get too taxing
One has one's little villa in Corfu
One owns one's piece of Perthshire
When one feels like just relaxing
One isn't short of places to go
One isn't short of things to do, but . . .

Knightsbridge is nice
England incarnate
Jewel of the crown
Who'd live in Barnet?
Round the world cruising's
Terribly amusing
But when it comes to choosing
Who'd go to Birmingham?
When Knightsbridge is so nice.

Switzerland is superb for skiing and salting away
Your savings, whereas Scotland is significant for
Shooting in secluded surroundings, stalking stags
And socialising in scintillating scenery.
And the smoked salmon's simply super!
One seldom sojourns in Scandinavia, it's scarcely
Central to the social scene. Denmark's as dreary as
A dairy, the Swedes are servile sycophants, the Finns
Are fishy, and Norway's next to nowhere! And Cynthia
Says the Scandinavians all
Scamper around in the scuddy.
Spain's been spoilt by the smelly socks, the Smiths
From Salford or some similar slum, sullying the sands
With their snivelling siblings, sipping their Sangria
And sunning their skins. Sickening socialist scum.

Knightsbridge is nice
'Andy for 'Arrods
Knightsbridge is nice
'Part from the Arabs
'Ackney is 'orrible
Putney's pathetic
Shoreditch is shitty
'Ow I miss the Old Kent Road
But Knightsbridge is nice
Nice class of people
Ladies and gents
Seen through the peep-'ole
'Endon is 'ellish
Ealing is Polish
Greenwich is garbage
'Ow I miss the North-End Road.

It's better than shovelling shit in Sheffield
Better than bein' a brickie in Brixton
Better than coughin' in Clacton carryin' coal.
Better than makin' mops in Macclesfield
Beats bein' a bum in a boozer in Bermondsey
Better than down in a dump in
Dagenham, Dorking, Tooting, Barking, West Ham,
East Ham, Beckenham, Sydenham, drawin' your dole.

Finchley is foul
Clapham is common
Dulwich is dull
Lambeth is lousy
Tooting is tacky
Peckham is poxy
Just where is Watford?
Somewhere near Birmingham.

VIVE LA DIFFERENCE

Vive la différence
It's truly magnifique
    I have my yacht in St. Tropez
And mine's in Mozambique
    We're both completely different
We're both of us unique
    If both of us were just the same
    It really would be bleak
Vive la différence
It's quite extraordinaire
    You have your house in Kensington
While mine's in Eaton Square
    Though neither of us drink in pubs
    We both belong to different clubs
I was a captain in the Engineers
    And I was a major in the Grenadiers
Vive la différence
It's really de rigueur
    Well after all you are an earl
And I'm a simple sir!
    Vive la différence
    You know it's comme il faut
Our tailors' shops are miles apart
Though both in Savile Row
I like champagne, Veuve Cliquot
    I prefer Böllinger, don't you know
Give me a Bentley
I'll show you a car
    I prefer a Rolls by far
I like fishing
    I like hunting
I like rowing
    I like punting
Vive la différence
Between the day and night
Between the sunshine and the rain
Between the black and white
Vive la différence
The old world and the new
Between the pleasure and the pain
The Arab and the Jew

Vive la différence
Comme ci, comme ça toujours!
Between the humble and the vain
Between the rich and poor
Vive la différence
How dull the world would be
If everybody was the same
The same as you and me
Variety's the spice of life
    I quite agree
    I think
    Je pense
Well dammit all we're different
    So vive la différence

David Hicks and David Anderson
in *The Crack*　　　Photo Anthony Brannan

HARD ON THE OUTSIDE
COLD ON THE INSIDE

Got on my walkman
Playin' it loud
Don't care nothin' for my ear drums
Me and my walkman
I'm young and I'm proud
Take no garbage from the old bums
Hard on the outside
Cold on the inside

Listenin' to Motorhead
That's what I like
Don't like nobody respectable
Me and my girlfriend
On my motorbike
She got no brains but she's delectable
Warm on the outside
Zilch on the inside

Tell your momma that you won't be back
You're runnin' away with the leader of the pack
You don't care nothin' for your homework now
You ain't goin' back to school
You gonna be super cool
What good is it anyhow?

Out on the highway
Me and my gang
Ridin' faster than the Valkyrie
Livin' for just today
Me and my gang
Twentieth century Samurai
Hard on the outside
Cold on the inside

Don't let nobody get in our way
We'll hack you down as soon as look at you
We'll stop at nothin' to get our way
We won't think twice about beheading you
'Cos we're the merchants of death
We're colder than ice
Before you take your last breath
Take a look in the eyes
Of the heavy metal team
See what I mean?

It's not my walkman
Ain't got a bike
Ain't got a hope in hell of gettin' one
But when you are thirteen
That's what you like
Fantasies of bein' someone
Hard on the outside
Cold on the inside

A MARVELLOUS DINNER

We had a marvellous dinner
The finest wine
The richest fare
We started with a nightingale
That used to sing in Berkeley Square
Cooked to a turn
Just a little rare

We had a wonderful dinner
One only had
One canapé
We followed with the tongue of a lark
Who rose a little late one day
Only the tongue
He must have got away

The veal was bled
Till the flesh was white
The beef was red
And the pastry light
The Stilton blue
The Chartreuse green
The aubergines were aubergine

Myra McFadyen
in *The Crack*
Photo Anthony Brannan

We had an exquisite dinner
With every course
A different wine
We started with a Liebfraumilch
From our vineyard on the river Rhine
Then a Bordeaux
That was too divine
The port was warm
The champagne dry
I forget the fish
Tho' I can't think why
The deer got dead
Just the other night
One loves a beast who puts up a fight

We had a sumptuous dinner
The silver gleamed
In the candlelight
The centrepiece was monkey's brains
I nearly came with every bite
Jolly good show
Just like every night
We had a marvellous dinner
Thank you so much

HEAR THE CRACK

Squeeze the stone until it bleeds
Scythe down the broken reeds
Show no mercy
Show no pity
Blood and thunder in the city
Screw the thumb
Stretch the rack
Let them feel it on their back
Let them hear the whiplash crack
Hear the crack
Hear the crack

Grind the nose and turn the stone
Singe the flesh and break the bone
Don't be timid
Little girlies
Grab them by the short and curlies
Gouge and claw
Rip and hack
Burn and murder, loot and sack
Then we'll hear resistance crack
Hear it crack
Hear it crack

Use the army, use the state
Bloody well exterminate
Those who struggle
Those who battle
Round them up like sheep and cattle
Taff and Tim
Mick and Mac
Rastafarian and black
Let them hear the rifle crack
Hear it crack
Hear it crack

We will never hand it over
We're in clover, we're all right Jack
If you want to take it from us
Only your force will make us crack
Hold on, hold on

Did you think we'd disappeared?
Were no longer to be feared?
Obsolescent
Superseded
That our magic had receded
We've the guile
We've the knack
We can always claw it back
Paper over any crack
That's the crack
That's the crack

Gerry Mulgrew
in *Business in the Backyard*

Photo Tom Hilton

BUSINESS IN THE BACKYARD

On 19 July 1979, the people of Nicaragua freed
themselves from one of the most corrupt and bloody
dictatorships in the history of Latin America and thereby set
an example which will one day be followed by the rest of the
continent. Si Nicaragua Venció, El Salvador Vencerá! On
the opening night of this show at the Pavilion Theatre in
Glasgow, the Nicaraguan Ambassador thanked the people
of Scotland from the stage, for their continuing support and
asked us to share with them in their hopes and in their
dreams. Nicaragua's struggle has struck a deep vein of
sympathy and solidarity in Scotland, perhaps because we,
too, know how all pervasive the American influence can be,
and how dangerous it would become if it turned into open
hostility.

Again, the people we could thank for helping us to
research and mount the production would fill another book,
but we will mention three representative names: Sister Mary
Isabel Kilpatrick SND, who told us of her own experiences
in Nicaragua and introduced us to the Misa Campesina,
John Gillies, who spent long hours translating source
material from the Spanish and Mike Gonzalez, whose
knowledge of the history and poetry of Central America was
invaluable.

We are still watching you, U.S.A. . . . don't even think
about it.

A HUNDRED FIRES

WAKE UP DOLORES

Wake up Dolores
The warm wind is sighing
The children are crying
Wake up Dolores

Wake up Dolores
The village is waking
It's time to be baking
Wake up Dolores

Wake up Dolores
There's no time for dreaming
The baby is screaming
Wake up Dolores

Tortillas Dolores
Tortillas Dolores
Tortillas Dolores

THE WAY THE RIVER RUNS

From the depths of the mysterious world
God sends up a tiny fountain
Through the rocks of countless centuries
To spring to light high up on the mountain
And the spring becomes a rivulet
The rivulet becomes a stream
And the stream runs down to the river
And the river runs by the village
That's the way the river runs

And every morning at the crack of dawn
Someone has to fetch the water
From the river that runs down through El Salvador
To cook the bread to feed the campesinos

Dolores which is sorrows
Cienfuegos which is a hundred fires
Dolores Cienfuegos
Which is the sorrow of a hundred fires

Somewhere on the mountain in a village
By the river in El Salvador
Cienfuegos is the family in the village
By the river in El Salvador

The hundred fires are the stars above
A hundred eyes that shine with love
A hundred eyes that brim with tears
On mortal men with mortal fears
Nicolas Saint of Christmas
Cienfuegos which is a hundred fires
Nicolas Cienfuegos
Which is Christmas of a hundred stars
Nicolas is the dreamer in the family
In the village in El Salvador
Nicolas Saint of Christmas is the
Poet in the family Cienfuegos

The hundred fires are the fires we light
When first we learn to stand and fight
A hundred fires to set us free
A hundred fires for liberty
Guerrita which means warrior
Cienfuegos which is a hundred fires
Guerrita Cienfuegos
Which means the warrior of a hundred fires
My namesake Camilo Cienfuegos
Came down from the Sierra Maestra
In Cuba with Fidel and Ché and
Set fire to the Dictator Batista's
Tail — and we shall do the same here.

Fire in the people's blood
Fire in the people's heart

From the hundred fires
In the infinite sky
To the infinitesimal fire
Of the fire fly
In the tiniest breath
Of the air that we breathe
In the spaces between us
In the wind's sigh

God is in the air
God is in the air

The hundred fires are the fires that burn
In all the villages that yearn
A hundred pleas for food and peace
That all our suffering will cease
Consuelo is consolation
Cienfuegos is a hundred fires
Consuelo Cienfuegos
The consolation of a hundred fires
And the river joins the people of the village
To their neighbours in El Salvador
And the river brings the news of every
fireside by the river in El Salvador
When I go to fetch water
I see reflected in the river
All the faces of the people of El Salvador
The river takes my tears down into the sea
That's the way the river runs

The hundred fires are the fires I build
To keep the children's bellies filled
A hundred hungry children cry
A thousand hungry children die
Dolores knows the sorrow
In the embers of a hundred fires
Dolores sees the future
In the ashes of a hundred fires
Hunger is the master in the family
In the village in El Salvador
There is plenty for the master but there's
Hunger for the many in El Salvador

That's the way the river runs
That's the way the river runs

God is in the air
God is in the air

Fire in the people's blood
Fire in the people's heart.

THE BARRIO

Camilo, Mercedes, Guillermo, Goodbye.
Maria, Manuel, Teresa, Goodbye.
And say goodbye to the country sky,
To the friends I know, say I'll always remember.
I've got to go to the barrio.

Down the track, through the woods, by the fields, I go
Round the bend, out of sight of the place I know.
And travel down to the edge of town
With no friends at all, where I'll just be a number
Looking for work in the barrio.

In the shanty town
Everywhere you go
There's no work around.
We have sunk so low
There's shacks made
Of old plastic crates from the Coca Cola plant,
But you can't get a job there,
You can't find work anywhere,
Down in the barrio.
It's just the same
In San Salvador.
We're just as poor
As the home I remember,
Starving to death in the barrio.

THE MISSING
(From an idea by Myra McFadyen)

When you sent your child to school today
Can you remember what she wore?
Try to keep that image, as she left you, in your head.

Was she wearing ribbons?
What colour were the ribbons?
Helps to make it easy to identify the dead.

Silent women
Carry pictures
Faded photos
Of the missing
Hoping you'll recognise someone.
Have you seen her?
Have you seen him?
Here's a picture
Can you help me?
Thousands of innocents have gone.

A sea of ghosts still fighting for their land.
From the lost to the living close at hand.
Will you remember faces?
Will you remember names?
Not a whisper
To the stranger
Must be silent
We're in danger
Of joining the thousands who have gone.
Not a murmur
They may kill us.
Passing stranger
Can you help us?
Think of your daughters and your sons.
Silently we commemorate the dead
Asking you to say what can't be said.
Will you remember faces?
Will you remember names?

BUSINESS IN THE BACKYARD

Business in the backyard
Booming although times are hard
Money somehow comes my way
Business in the backyard
I'm in business, buddy, here's my card
God bless me and the National Guard

On the news tonight
We heard the President
Speaking live from Washington D.C.
Give the blessing of the Government
On El Salvador's democracy

Down South
In the backyard
We keep out of sight
To make sure the backyard
Stays right
Way down
In the backyard
It's so far away
Guess who's
In the backyard
It's the C.I.A.!

Business in the backyard
Booming 'cos we work real hard
So it's gonna stay that way
We say from the backyard
Don't you pay us no regard
God bless you and the National Guard

From the top of the mountain
The stream runs down to the river
Nothing on earth can stop the river
Running down into the sea

And the sea becomes an ocean
Joins the oceans over all the world
Joins the rivers over all the world
Joins the countries and the people
That's the way the river runs
That's the way the river runs
That's the way the river runs
That's how surely the people will be free
The way the river runs

The Company
in *Business in the Backyard*
Photo Tom Hilton

Rab Handleigh, David Anderson and David Hicks
in *It's a Free Country*
Photo Oscar Marzaroli

IT'S A FREE COUNTRY

A return to 'Beggars' Cabaret' — albeit these beggars wore some fairly snappy 'tin flutes'. But the suits, like the times, only glittered on the surface. Stuart Mungall, who is not afraid of using scissors if material of the written kind fails to glitter, directed. The result was a night which fairly rattled along.

The Beggars' Band welcomed to its ranks Neil Hay on bass and Gordon Dougall on guitar. Terry Neason returned to sing some more telephone directories in Gregorian plain chant! New scribblers were Peter Arnott with some very funny sketches and Marcella Evaristi with a beautiful ballad.

The erosion of civil liberties during the miners' strike of 1984–85 had been fairly spectacular, with the police assuming powers that nobody knew they possessed and many doubted they should. Wildcat's life has more or less coincided with the Thatcher Government's tenure of office, and a fairly depressing experience it has been. The challenge has been to reflect the struggles of our audience to protect themselves from the Tories' more hostile actions, to give public expression to their hopes and fears, their dreams and their nightmares, but to do it in a way which helps them to carry on the fight rather than reaching for the switch of the gas oven!

Terry Neason and David Anderson
in *It's a Free Country*
Photo Oscar Marzaroli

POLICE SONG
(To the tune "Galway Bay")

Have you ever been across the sea to Belfast
And seen the way the Police force operate?
Well now we've got the same thing on the mainland
We never want another Saltley Gate.

Since Kenneth Newman came across from Belfast
We've got the things we need to keep the peace
'Ello, 'ello, 'ello, what's all this, then
Suddenly we've got the National Police.

JINGO

The magic of Jingo
Is powerful Ju Ju
It come from the Gringo
Is better than Voodoo
We speaka da lingo
We tell you what to do
Hoodoo!
You do right
Is sweeter than mango
Is bigger than Ringo
We set up a Quango
You go to the Bingo
We dance a fandango
You bark like a dingo
Hoodoo!
You do right
Jingo
Jingo

When the world ain't going right
And people feel you're doing wrong
When you think you've lost the fight
Don't give up, you must be strong
When the world's on Red Alert
And they just don't trust you guys
If the truth is gonna hurt
Simply tell them lies

When you've been discredited
In some country in the East
No matter how you edited
Somehow the facts have got released
When the boys who had to go
Wonder what they did it for
Make a movie just to show
How you won the war.

The power of Jingo
Gonna get you
The power of Jingo
Gonna get you
Jingo
Jingo
Gonna get to you

The magic of Jingo
Is powerful Ju Ju
It come from the Gringo
Is better than Voodoo
We speaka da lingo
We tell you what to do
Hoodoo!
You do right
Is sweeter than mango
Is bigger than Ringo
We set up a Quango
You go to the Bingo
You dance a fandango
You bark like a dingo
Hoodoo!
You do right
Jingo
Jingo

NO, CINDERELLA

In a portakabin classroom
In a poorer part of town
Sits a portakabin princess
And her eyes are gazing down
For the view beyond the window
Fills the princess full of fears
And the posters on the cabin wall
Fill the princess's eyes with tears.

It used to be the teacher
Put their paintings on the walls
Cottages with garden paths
Children kicking balls
Rockets, planes and submarines
Racing cars and battle scenes
Witches wearing pointed hats
With purple dogs and yellow cats
The stuff of fantasies and dreams
That each day
They would play
Far away
From the housing schemes.

But now the posters on the wall
Say 'Drug Abuse' and 'Alcohol'
And the most important one of all
Tells the portakabin princess
To go forthwith to the D.H.S.S.
And not as she hoped to the ball.

And your supermarket jeans
Won't become a sequinned gown
And the clips that hold your hair up
Won't become a silver crown
And the sneakers on your feet
Won't be made of glass
And at midnight it will only be
Another day passed.

The car the kids have wrecked
Won't become a gilded coach
And the rats won't turn to footmen
Who will bow when you approach
And the dogs that roam the streets
Won't be ponies for the day
And Buttons will be what you get on Giro Day.

No, Cinderella,
You're not going to the ball.

And the band won't play in the hut tonight
You can't have a dance since the last big fight
And there'll be no prince to hold you tight
No crystal slipper that fits just right.
And the crowd won't see in the candlelight
How the princess's eyes are shining bright
No champagne toast, no grouse, no trout
No one to tell you you're erudite.

No, Cinderella,
You're not going to the ball.

Your journey will be to the buroo
No coach -and-four, a bus for you
Perhaps you'll leg it in the rain
Your ball will be a ball and chain
Your prince will be a counter clerk
You'll travel home long after dark
Your palace on the thirteenth floor
Will have no roses round the door.

And you're not going to be a prince's wife
'Cos you're not cut out for that kind of life
And you'll get run down on the yellow brick road
And the frog you kiss will become a toad
And the wicked witch and the forty thieves
Gonna get rich quick on the spell she weaves
And you may be cute and you may be blonde
But she'll cut you down with her magic wand.

No, Cinderella,
You're not going to the ball.

And the Court will sleep for a hundred years
But a week is a long time in politics.

Terry Neason and Neil Hay
in *It's a Free Country*
Photo Oscar Marzaroli

ARMAGEDDON

You insurrectionist
in your squalid room
damned godless communist
prepare to meet thy doom
for the army of anger
and hatred awaits the command
and the jealous Jehovah has judged
you must fall where you stand
for the day of the great and the
grand and the grave is at hand
                    is at hand

You evolutionist
under the stairs
anti-creationist
say your prayers
for the wrath of the righteous is
ready to rain on your head
and the angels of vengeance
are coming to drag you from bed
it's the guys with the guns
and the boys will rejoice when you're dead
                    when you're dead

Burn, baby, burn
you who failed to read the writing on the wall
turn, baby, turn
insurrection's this direction after all
we're comin' to
interview
you know who

You unilateralist
weak liberal scum
you with the limp wrist
gonna blow you to kingdom come
for the power and the glory
is ours on the day that you die
and the lust of the just's for the fire
in which you're gonna fry
so before you go down
to your hole in the ground, say goodbye
                    say goodbye

WILDNIGHTS AT THE TRON

This was a co-production with the Glasgow Theatre Club, and our first Christmas show. Something for the weary Glaswegian to visit after taking the kids to see all the pantos!

The taste for variety and the Music Hall is alive and well in the West of Scotland, and this motley of Wildcat songs and sketches, a review of the year and some of the best local acts, brought the punters in their droves. They liked Bing Hitler, and they liked the Glasgow Asian Dancers, they laughed with Arnold Brown and with Liz Lochhead. Juliet Cadzow did a one act Dario Fo/Franca Rame play to their great delight, Two and Two makes Sax played swing and Rab Noakes sung folk, and a great many others on the burgeoning cabaret scene performed nightly in an atmosphere which had not been seen since the seedy days of the Weimar Republic.

OUT WITH THE OLD

The clock strikes midnight
And everybody cheers
The hugging and the kissing
The laughter and the tears
We get so sentimental
We drink to absent friends
We're nice to one another
We hope it never ends
We made it
We made it once again

Out with the old
Cold
Feeling
Out with the old
Cold
Blues
In with the new you
The one you've been concealing
Out with the old, in with the new

And Daddy's body-poppin'
And Grandma sings the blues
And junior's moon-walking
And Uncle hits the juice
And everybody party!
The wine is goin' fast
So get it while it's goin'
It isn't gonna last
We made it, so let's forget the past.

D'you make a resolution?
One you're gonna keep?
Gonna cut your drinking
Before you get too deep?
Gonna give up smokin
Before you wind up dead?
Gonna build a future
Where Angels fear to tread?
We can do it
Gotta get it through my head

Out with the old
Cold
Feeling
Out with the old
Cold
Blues
In with the new you
The one you've been concealing
Out with the old, in with the new.

HEATHER UP YOUR KILT

A farce set in the cocktail bar of the Clachan Dhu Hotel, somewhere near Dunoon — or was it Brigadoon? Robert Roy MacGregor and his beautiful but icy wife Denise are visiting from their native Oregon — tracing their roots. Why is the local malt whisky blue? Could it be anything to do with the explosion at the Olympus Research Establishment? This show was a kind of "An American in Harris."

In order to keep her visitors in this ecological disaster area where no tourists have been seen for months, Heather Smith — alias "MacGregor" — the general dogsbody at the Clachan Dhu and the sole remaining inhabitant of Bonnyburn — well, apart from Tam who seems to be in some sort of catatonic trance — Heather, remember Heather? — impersonates almost the whole of the clan MacGregor, including Sir Gregor MacGregor of MacGregor of that Ilk, and . . . oh never mind, that's what happens when you try to describe the plot of a farce.

It provided a good vehicle for the quick change artistry of Myra McFadyen, and in it we tried to answer such questions as: Is Scotland's greatest cultural achievement the tartan tin of shortbread petticoat tails, and does a small nation have the right to self-determination?

Steven Wren, Myra McFadyen and Blythe Duff
in *Heather up your Kilt*
Photo Alan Wylie

AN AMERICAN IN HARRIS

When I was a little boy
Grampa sat me on his knee
He said "Son, you're only wee
But one day you'll go across the sea
To the old country
Bonnie Scotland
Where the Lassies sure are bonnie
And you won't need any money
When they hear your name
In your hielan' hame
They'll say 'bide a wee by the fire'

There will be a sheiling
And a cosy ingle too
Where the bonnie coos will moo
As if to say 'And how are you the noo?'
In the old country
Bonnie Scotland"
And I'll see the braw big laddies
As the boats bring in the haddies
From the Irish Sea
And they'll wave at me
Sayin' "bide a wee by the harbour"

Bonnie Scotland
A stone's throw from Heaven
Where the livin'
Is braw and folks are simple
Bonnie Jeannie
McIntyre
In the byre
And her darling dimple

As the sun sets on the hillside
And the sheep are in the fold
There's a piece of ass worth more than gold
"Will you stop your ticklin', Jock", she'll scold
In the old country
Bonnie Scotland
Well it may sound cockamamie
But I'll know that hame'll dae me
And I'm no awa'
Fur tae bide awa'
For the sake of old lang zine
How I yearn to see that old country of mine

Steven Wren
in *Heather up your Kilt*
Photo Alan Wylie

Rab Handleigh and Myra McFadyen
in *Heather up your Kilt*
Photo Alan Wylie

TAM'S SONG

Well I was born one mornin' in the Gallowgate
To the sound of a lullaby
It was my Momma croonin' like Rosemary Clooney
To Mickey Rooney when he was a G.I.
My Grandpa played Ain't Misbehavin'
My Daddy sang the Little White Cloud (That Cried)
And my sister did impressions of Brenda Lee
I'll say it loud, now, I'm funky and proud

I found my thrill
On the radio
Hear that piano playin' in triple time
Long Tall Sally was a nursery rhyme
Who sang Eeny-Meeny and Miny-Mo?
Fats Domino

Don't talk to me about folk music
Don't talk to me about art
Don't talk to me about Andy Stewart
I know what I feel in my heart
I gotta right to sing the blues if I want to
Learned how to do it on my Grandma's knee
If it's good enough for Grandma it's good enough for me
You could say it runs in the family
And I like it, like it, yes I do

God bless America
For givin' us rhythm and blues
Jeepers Creepers
High-heel sneakers
Whatever they are
Chubby Checker
Desmond Dekker
No, he was Jamaican
Whatever happened to Tommy Tucker?
I remember when
We heard the Drifters play
Under the Board Walk
Behind the bike shed
And then she let me

I just called to say . . .
Stevie Wonder I love you
You move me to my very soul
I love all the Jacksons, especially Mahalia
Believe I was born to rock and roll
I'm not ashamed to admit it
I like it better than Ae Fond Kiss
I say thanks to my black brothers and sisters
For makin' me feel like this

Don't blame it on the multi-nationals
Or the imperialist Uncle Sam
Blame it on the boogie
Blame it on joy
Blame it on my grandma
When I was a boy
Blame it on the music that's made me the way I am

God bless America
For givin' us rhythm and blues
Keep your Dallas and your Dynasty
Your President, your foreign policy
I'll take Cagney and Lacey
Count Basie
Ray Charles
Even Spencer Tracey
But I'll say no dice
To Miami Vice
Give me your rhythm and blues
For which I love you

ALL-AMERICAN GIRL

If you look at a map of America
Take special notice of the State lines.
All the way from Norfolk, Virginia to Eureka, California
There's an awful lot of straight lines.
In the middle of the country —
I'm talkin' North Dakota, South Dakota, Nebraska,
Kansas, Oklahoma, Etcetera in particular.
In fact Wyoming and Colorada specifically are
Geographically peculiar.
I mean longitudinally and laterally
Horizontal and perpendicular
They are absolutely, literally, rectangular.
And every female child in this square new world
Just wants to be an all-American girl.

Every Saturday at the picture show
Up there upon the screen
In technicolor, cinemascope
Bobby-soxed and squeaky-clean
Her eyes were blue, her hair was blond
Her name was Doris Day.
Singin' please don't eat the daisies
She stole my heart away.
Skin like milk, teeth like pearls
Everybody loves an all-American girl.

Her Momma spends her day in the kitchen
Bakin' cookies and American pie.
They have cranberry sauce on Thanksgivin'
And a party on the Fourth of July.
Her Daddy comes home from the office
In a suit and an Ivy League tie.
She's gettin' married to a guy
Who cannot tell a lie.
It'll be a white wedding
Been in love since Junior High
She's so happy her head's in a whirl
She's so God-damn cute that all-American girl.

What you never see in movies
Is the wrong side of the tracks
Where there ain't no picket fences
Round the little beat-up shacks
Not a mile away from Doris Day
Where there ain't no blue-eyed cuties
In my neck of the boondocks
Just the black folks and the wet-backs
And the Injuns, Mr. Redneck,
Not a mile away from Doris Day
It's the very last place in the whole wide world
Where you're gonna find an all-American girl!

Not a mile away from Cosiville
There's another USA
Where the black folks and the Mexicans
And the Indians get to stay.
And I grew up in that hell-on-earth
Hopin' and prayin'
Knowin' that some day
I wouldn't be an Indian
And then I'd get away.
So I said I was white to the outside world
But I'll never be an all-American girl.

An all-American girl is the thing to be
If you wanna be happy in the land of the free.
So lie through your teeth to your mother-in-law
An all-American boy don't want no squaw.
You stole our country and you called it free.
You screwed our people, now you're screwin' me.

If you look at a map of America
Take special notice of the State lines
From the snows in the north to the sands of the south
There's an awful lot of straight lines.
The white man drew the boxes
on the land he took from the Sioux
From the Aztecs and the Eskimos
Screwed my people and now he's screwin' you.
And every TV screen in the whole wide world
Says the thing to be's an all-American girl
With her daddy's gun and her flag unfurled
But I'll never be an all-American girl.

Myra McFadyen
in *Heather up your Kilt*

Photo Alan Wylie

THE RIGHT OF NATIONS

Mr President
You tell me your war is holy
You're fighting the good fight
You tell me that God is on your side
And might is right.
We have to tell you we beg to differ
We don't like your attitude
It may be good for business
But it's doing us no good.

Did you hear about the last election?
We don't like our government
We don't like the way it goes through hoops
For the President.
We have to tell you we've got a message
So we're not misunderstood
It may be fine for London
But it doesn't suit our mood.

We're talkin' about a nation
Without representation
Needing liberation
From multi-national corporations.

You tell us you're just our ally
You're fighting on our side
It just feels like you're taking us
For one almighty ride.
We have to tell you we got a feeling
We can't win this steeplechase
You say you're bringing business
But you're shutting down the place.

We know all about your big ambitions
Just another US base.
When you want to strike you need somewhere,
We provide the place.
We have to tell you we got a message
So you don't misunderstand
The nuclear deterrent
We want the whole lot banned.

The whole population
Afraid of radiation
Or complete annihilation
From the installation.

We don't believe in Utopia
We'll face the actualities
It's not about political myopia
We're talking practicalities.
We're not nostalgic for the bad old days
Of which we've been bereft
It's a simple matter of a people
Who feel a lot more to the left.

The right of nations
To self-determination
The right of nations
To self-determination.
No more confrontation
And militarisation
Ecological pollution.
It's a practical solution
The right of nations
To self-determination.

JOTTERS

Education and unemployment seen through the eyes of the Mungos — your typical Glasgow family. Insofar as any family is typical. John Mungo, 45, a skilled engineer. Aristocracy of Labour. Unemployed. An aristocracy fallen on hard times. Wife Rosie, went to night classes and has now gone off to a craft village in the Hebrides with Penny the Potter from Paisley. Dangerous thing education, gives you ideas. Liz Mungo, late 20s, a secondary teacher at St. Jude's in the east end. Well named St. Jude's — patron saint of lost causes. Young John at the Uni. A psychologist researching into artificial intelligence. Then there's the twins, Jenny, a school leaver with a clutch of good highers, but just one point short for Medicine, and Davey on Y.T.S.

Jotters explores some of the popular myths of Scottish education, not least the most durable of them all, 'The myth of the lad o' pairts'. Well, there aren't too many kids from Easterhouse wandering the groves of academe with sacks of oatmeal on their backs. In fact more young people leave school in Scotland at the minimum legal age with no qualifications than in any other country in Europe. Not so — Portugal's worse! Oh well, that's O.K. then.

Gordon Dougall, Christina Zdanavich, Neil Hay, Lesley Robertson and David Anderson
in *Jotters*
Photo Alan Wylie

THE DESOLATE NORTH OF WATFORD

In the frozen North
In the snow and ice
Not a creature stirs
In the grip of winter's vice.
And the rivers freeze
When the blizzards blow
And the city sleeps
In the drifting winter snow.
Then a pale winter sun
Brings a bleak winter dawn
All the swallows have flown
And the winding gear stands
Silent guard on the landscape
In the desolate North of Watford.

See the shipyard crane
Frozen in its track
Not a furnace flames
All the forges cold and black.
Seems the great white heat
Must have passed them by
Sunrise industry
Never even lit the sky.
And it wasn't the North
But the South wind brought snow
And the South wind doth blow
And no robin can stand
On the cold Northern landscape
In the desolate North of Watford.

Wouldn't it be nice
Just to stay in bed
For a moment more
Pull the downie round your head.
Sleep, perchance to dream
Dream, perhaps of sun
Sun, maybe this year
When the winter's come and gone.
But the thin winter wind
Chills you right to the bone
How much colder its grown
Since the ice maiden's hand
Brushed and wintered the landscape
In the desolate North of Watford.

Lesley Robertson
in *Jotters*
Photo Alan Wylie

JENNY'S SONG

Some day soon when school is out
Tell me what you're gonna be.
Used to be that there was no doubt
Be what I wanna be.
I studied hard and I wrote real neat
You bored me stiff and I acted sweet.
And now that I can see the winning post
You pull the rug from my feet.
And now you say you don't want me, oh no
And now you say you don't want me.

Work real hard get an easy ride
Seventeen and gullible.
Must have seen I came up the Clyde
Ridin' on a bicycle.
Now you say I'm under-qualified
And I can't win no matter how I tried.
Why don't you aim a little lower, baby
And swallow your pride?
Now you say I can't make it, oh no
Now you say I can't make it.

And you don't need what I've got to offer you
Tho' you needed it a moment ago.
You told me lies and I trusted you
One day you love me and the next I'm through.
You don't want me and it seems to me
Don't want nobody in my family.
Don't want nobody in my neck of the woods
Or in the neighbouring neighbourhoods
Or in the city population
Come to think, do you need the nation?

One day soon something's gonna give
There's gonna be a reckoning.
You don't need us but we gotta live
You'll know it when it's happening.
You'll feel the anger you've been storin' up
The dam'll burst that you've been shorin' up.
You'll have to listen good to us
Instead of just ignorin' us.
And we will say we don't need you, oh no
And we will say we don't need you.

The Company Rehearsal
Photo Tom Hilton

DAVID ANDERSON

Born '45 in Rutherglen, into large family in small house. Learned piano from three generations of family. Joined first band at fifteen. Spent more than earned from rock 'n' roll in Scotland, then left for Canada at twenty-one. Bummed around North America for three years before returning and going straight to London for five years, playing in bands and solo work in clubs, restaurants etc., writing songs all the while.

Returned to Scotland for three months in 1974. Been here ever since, learning something about theatre from John McGrath and the remarkable players of early 7:84. Kept saying, "Aye, O.K." to MacLennan at inception of Wildcat, now finds he's a 'founder member'. Wrote/co-wrote the songs contained here. Incidentally and fortuitously, has carried on a film/T.V. acting career; e.g. *Gregory's Girl*, *Heavenly Pursuits* etc., *City Lights* sit-com for BBC Scotland.

Married. Two children. Lives in Maryhill, Glasgow.

Photo Alan Crumlish

DAVID MACLENNAN

Born '48 in Glasgow. Small family, large house. Just a wee joke. Gave up piano lessons. Played washboard in skiffle group, aged eight. Lonnie Donegan songs. Educated in various boarding schools, left aged sixteen thoroughly inoculated against the system of private education. Early career as hospital porter and taxi driver interrupted by two years studying politics at Edinburgh University, followed by eighteen months as Edinburgh Corporation bin man. First job in the theatre in Brighton in 1969 as assistant stage manager.

Joined 7:84 when it started in 1971 and later the Scottish 7:84 in 1973 for *The Cheviot* . . . Worked at that time with John McGrath, John Arden, Trevor Griffiths and many other good writers, actors and musicians. Wrote three shows for 7:84 before helping to start Wildcat. Their first show was *The Painted Bird* and since then they've done another twenty-one. The lyrics in this book were written for these shows. Wrote first song with Anderson in 1975 and the output shows no sign of abating.

Divorced. No children. Lives in Blackfriars Street, Glasgow.

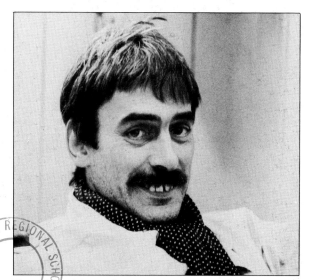

Photo Oscar Marzaroli

82

LIST OF WILDCAT PRODUCTIONS IN
CHRONOLOGICAL ORDER

Autumn '78	THE PAINTED BIRD by David MacLennan and David Anderson	
Spring '79	THE COMPLETE HISTORY OF ROCK 'N' ROLL by David McNiven and David Anderson	
Autumn '79	DUMMIES by David MacLennan and David Anderson	
Spring '80	THE BARMECIDE FEAST by David McNiven	
Autumn '80	BLOOTER by David MacLennan and David Anderson	
Spring '81	CONFESSIN' THE BLUES by David Anderson and company	
Autumn '81	HOT BURLESQUE by David McNiven	
Spring '82	1982 by David MacLennan and David Anderson	
Autumn '82	HIS MASTER'S VOICE by David Anderson	
Spring '83	BUNCH OF FIVES by David Anderson, Sean Hardie, Tom Leonard, Liz Lochhead, David MacLennan	
Autumn '83	WELCOME TO PARADISE by David Anderson	
Spring '84	BED-PAN ALLEY by David MacLennan and David Anderson	

Summer '84   SAME DIFFERENCE
by Liz Lochhead

Autumn '84   DEAD LIBERTY
by David MacLennan and David Anderson

Spring '85   THE CRACK
by David Anderson and David MacLennan

Summer '85   BUSINESS IN THE BACK YARD
by David MacLennan and David Anderson

Autumn '85   IT'S A FREE COUNTRY
by David Anderson, Peter Arnott, Gordon Dougall, Marcella Evaristi, Rab Handleigh, Tom Leonard, Terry Neason, David MacLennan

Christmas '85   WILDNIGHTS AT THE TRON
by David Anderson, Peter Arnott, Tom Leonard, David MacLennan

Spring '86   THE BEGGAR'S OPERA OR PEACHUM'S POORHOUSE
by David MacLennan and David MacNiven

Summer '86   HEATHER UP YOUR KILT
by David Anderson and David MacLennan

Christmas '86   A WILDCAT CHRISTMAS CAROL
by Peter Arnott

Spring '87   JOTTERS
by David MacLennan and David Anderson

INDEX OF SONGS